Japanese Business Concepts You Should Know

Edited by Parissa Haghirian
Professor of International Management

Sophia University
Tokyo, Japan

Contents

About this Book 3

The Editor.. 4

Japanese Busines Concepts You Should Know 6

Contributors of This Book 300

Bibliography 302

Further Reading on Japanese Management........... 312

About this Book

This book is the result of one of my "Management in Japan" classes held at the Faculty of Liberal Arts at Sophia University in Tokyo. Students wrote this dictionary entries, I edited and updated them.

We hope that this book improves understanding of Japanese management and serves as inspiration for anyone interested in the subject.

Questions and comments can be sent to japanesebusinessconcepts@haghirian.com. Please inform the editor if you plan to quote parts of the book.

Japanese Business Concepts You Should Know
Edited by Parissa Haghirian
First Paperback Edition
Tokyo, September 2020

The Editor

Parissa Haghirian is Professor of International Management at Sophia University, Tokyo. She has lived and worked in Japan since 2004 and is an internationally renowned expert in international management with a focus on Japanese management.

Professor Haghirian studied Japanese Studies at the University of Vienna (MA 1999) and holds a master's degree (2000) and PhD in Business Administration (2003) from the Vienna University of Economics and Business Administration. She is also a visiting professor at Aalto University, HEC Paris, Keio University, Waseda University, and the University of Vienna. From 2011 to 2012 she held a professorship in Japanese Management at Ludwig-Maximilians-Universität München (LMU).

She has published several books and articles on the topic of Japanese management, and is the author of *Understanding Japanese Management Practices* (Business Expert Press, 2010), *Multinationals and Cross-Cultural Management: The Transfer of Knowledge Within Multinational Corporations* (Routledge, 2010) and *Successful Cross-cultural Management: a Guide for International Managers* (Business Expert Press, 2011). She is also the editor of *Japanese Consumer Dynamics* (Palgrave Macmillan 2011), *Case Studies in Japanese Management* (World Scientific Publishing Company, 2011), the *Routledge Handbook of Japanese Business and Management* (Routledge, 2016) and *Business Development, Merger and Crisis Management of International Firms in Japan: Featuring Case Studies from Fortune 500 Companies* (World Scientific Publishing Company, 2018).

Professor Haghirian advises companies on intercultural cooperation, and coaches top-level managers searching for new perspectives and the potential for success. She regularly gives keynote lectures at conferences and corporate events across Europe and Asia. She currently lives in Tokyo.

Contact
japanesebusinessconcepts@haghirian.com
www.haghirian.com

Japanese Business Concepts You Should Know

amae

甘え

Indulgent dependency

Behavior which shows your desire to be loved, your expectation that someone will take care of you, and your deep desire for acceptance— perhaps, even an unconscious desire for dependency, coupled with a degree of submissiveness—is characterized by *amae*. A person manifesting *amae* may beg or plead, or alternatively act selfishly and indulgently, all the while secure in the knowledge that the caregiver will forgive them. *amae*, then, signifies a wish for dependency, whether on one's family, partner, or boss.

Although *amae* may be found all over the world, Japanese culture emphasizes it particularly strongly—as reflected in the fact that the Japanese language assigns it a specific word. *amae* comes from the verb *amaeru*, meaning "to depend on the benevolence of others," "behave self-indulgently," or "to presume on some special relationship." *amae* is mostly shown to members of one's own group, and does not apply to strangers.

The psychoanalyst Doi Takeo has elaborated on this aspect of Japanese psychology. According to Doi, Japanese people do not feel comfortable or right in any relationship that does not include *amae*, which he defines as an indulgent dependency rooted in the mother–child bond. *amae* is experienced by the child as a feeling of dependency or a desire to be loved, while the mother experiences satisfaction and fulfillment through overindulgence and overprotectiveness of her child.

amae concerns the duties and sacrifices involved in belonging to a group. It is a strength of the group relationship, and plays a fundamental role in a collectivist society, as is the case in Japan, where group orientation is taken to be more important than individualism. A claim of *amae* is a claim of dependence. It often occurs when one first joins a company or school, where a person must quickly get integrated into a comfortable niche. The subordinate gets a channel through which to move upward; the superior gets someone to do their bidding; and, within the group, success is shared by all and guilt is diffused when something goes wrong.

amae assists the process of creating harmonious interconnections within families, in companies, and between friends. Japanese do not usually confront each other, and it is very rare to see Japanese people arguing. *amae* is one of the tools which maintains this harmony.

amae has many different manifestations and can be found everywhere: at home, in education and work relationships, in *manga* (漫画) and *anime* (アニメ), in Japanese pop music, etc. It is also relevant to business negotiations, where Japanese are more comfortable when they can identify the superior individual, who is expected to show benevolence and give concessions to the junior. It is interesting, though, to see how roles can be reversed during the negotiation process when it is the superior party who has to ask for concessions.

Within a company, *amae* is an important part of the senior–junior relationship. In such pairings, the individual in the senior position expects the junior to accept unreasonable demands; meanwhile, the junior can expect help, indulgence, or forgiveness from the superior. Both presume some special relationship between them. A further example is the *senpai–kōhai* (先輩—後輩) relationship. The *senpai* is considered an older brother who is supposed to give guidance and show benevolence toward the *kōhai*. (J.B.)

See also: *senpai-kōhai, awase, giri, ganbaru and gaman*

amakudari

天下り

Heaven descent

In its narrow sense, *amakudari* refers to the practice of providing top government officials with elite, high-paying jobs in private corporations after they retire. In a broader sense, it refers to two career paths available after retirement: entering public corporations, or the political arena. In their new positions, the former bureaucrats utilize their networks and insider knowledge from previous employment to maintain smooth relations with the ministries responsible for licensing and regulation. While *amakudari* is considered a central component of Japanese human management, recently this institution has come under criticism for being corrupt.

Literally translated, *amakudari* means "descent from heaven." Before World War II, civil servants believed they served the emperor, seen as a divine being that embodied every Japanese ideal. Working for the emperor was akin to being in heaven; the move from the public to the private sector marked one's descent.

While *amakudari* has historical roots in the Meiji period, it wasn't until after World War II that it became institutionalized. Before the war, positions for retirees were individually negotiated; post-war, the secretariat's office main responsibility became arranging jobs for bureaucrats, who were forced to retire by their early fifties. Faced with the need to respect the institutions of early retirement, lifetime employment, and seniority, *amakudari* was the perfect solution. In this sense, *amakudari* directly stems from the existence of these post-war institutions. Within a few years, the secretariat's office had complete control over the best positions in the private sector. From 1949–1959 *amakudari* and *yokosuberi* (横滑り or sideways shift to another post) accounted for over 60% of post-retirement jobs.

From a ministerial perspective, *amakudari* provides deferred compensation for civil servants, as well as enabling surveillance of private corporations. For government bureaucrats, obtaining an *amakudari* job is often equivalent to a promotion. These positions are highly sought after and intensely competitive, and so attract only the most talented personnel. *amakudari* thus provides the government with windows into the private sector, allowing the ministries to monitor them via their former staffers now working in senior private-sector positions.

From a corporate perspective, *amakudari* helps private companies stay competitive in the market, reduce risks, and form a mutual basis of trust. After they move to their new jobs, the former bureaucrats provide their companies with information that would otherwise have been inaccessible, allowing them to stay current with the ministry that is regulating them and adapt accordingly. This engenders greater efficiency and effectiveness.

Recently, *amakudari* has become a controversial media topic, seen increasingly as a corrupt practice that prevents Japan from implementing the major economic reforms it needs in order to move forward. But while many people want to try to ban or restrict the practice, *amakudari* is so intertwined in both private and public sectors that the prospects for change are dim. Many high-profile individuals in various dignified institutions throughout Japan support *amakudari* and will use their connections and influence to defend it. If change does occur, it will likely be a long time coming. (F.B.)

See also: *fuhai, gakubatsu, taishoku*

anzen

安全

Safety

The concept of *anzen*—safety—is intertwined with Japanese management systems. In Japan it goes without saying that a worker's health is inextricable from the quality of their performance. Health and safety management systems are connected to a company's production system, and methods and techniques are developed in order to ensure the safety of workers by reference to the protocols of organizations such as the Japan Industrial Safety & Health Association (JISHA).

The aphorism *anzen nakushite seisan nashi*— "without safety there can be no production"—speaks to a fundamental feature of the Japanese system of Just-in-Time (JIT) production. The point is not just that JIT requires workers to perform well at their workstations in order to ensure the quality of products and efficiency in production; more importantly, this system, which is meant to reduce costs by cutting down on inventories, is also vulnerable to greater losses should there be an accident that halts the production line. JIT production therefore requires that emphasis be placed on health and safety.

JISHA was established in 1964 with the aim of ensuring worker safety. In accordance with the Industrial Accident Prevention Organization Law, JISHA devised several programs to prevent accidents in the workplace. One of the most effective of these is the Zero-accident Total Participation Campaign (also known as the Zero-accident Campaign), initiated in 1973, which aims at the elimination of industrial accidents through the participation of all workers. The Zero-accident Campaign is built around three basic principles: zero accidents, preemptive action, and participation. Through preemptive action it is believed that hazards and accidents can be detected prior to occurrence and are thus preventable; participation entails the full and mutual commitment of employees and employers in the detection, understanding, and solving of potential workplace hazards.

The Zero-accident Campaign utilizes a number of programs, including the *kiken yochi* (危険予知) training (hazard prediction training or KYT). Applying this method on the production floor greatly decreases the chances of accidents and allows the company to perform at maximum efficiency. KYT can be seen as comprising four stages: in the first, workers understand their surroundings and take note of hidden hazards; in the second, having confirmed the locations of hazard points, workers inspect whether these points actually present dangers; in the third, workers are asked how they would react if they were confronted with these hazards, and how to devise counter measures; and, finally, workers establish the actual danger points and set targets concerning which points to avoid. With KYT, workers heighten their awareness of hazards and, working in groups, attempt to find solutions.

Another technique used in Japanese companies is "point and calling"; this method requires workers to identify a potential threat, point to it, and state out loud whether it is ok. This occurs at important work checkpoints to ensure safety as workers proceed. Workers attend meetings and are taught proper procedures so that they become fully aware of unsafe conditions or unsafe behavior in the workplace. When on the assembly line, workers are taught precise motion sequences in order to ensure maximum efficiency and avoid accidents. Finally, the toolbox meeting *kiken yochi*, a variation of the KYT, is a work group meeting that addresses common hazards. These meetings, usually of about three to fifteen minutes, allow employees to work together and come up with solutions to address hazards. It is believed that a worker's own personal safety and the safety of others around him can be achieved if KYT is applied correctly.

Safety cannot be fully achieved without the full participation of employees and managers. Japanese managers and employees are taught to always be on the look-out for hazards and ways to mitigate them. By applying the concept of *kaizen*, the process of continuous improvement, employees and managers constantly think of improvements to production, thus leading to improvements in health and safety. (A.C.)

See also: *Just-in-Time (JIT), kaizen*

Arubaito - freeter - haken

アルバイト - フリーター - 派遣

Part time work

In large Japanese firms, lifetime employment is a long-established practice and there is no doubt that it has been a force behind Japan's economic development. However, part-time workers make up a rising share of total employment. The most widespread examples of part-time employment in Japan are *arubaito*, *freeter*, and *haken*.

The word for part-time work, *arubaito*, is not a native Japanese term but a *gairaigo* (foreign loanword), derived from the German *Arbeit*, meaning work or labor. Employment for fewer hours than a full-time job, usually fewer than 30 or 35 hours per week, is considered part-time work. In Japan, *arubaito* primarily refers to part-time work undertaken by high school and college students. According to a survey by the Japan Youth Research Institute, nearly half of all Japanese high school students have done *arubaito* at one time or another. "Part-time" also can refer to students who take less than a full load of courses, and work simultaneously to earn money. High school students generally earn between 600 and 1,000 yen per hour, and the most common workplaces for high school and college students are fast-food restaurants, family restaurants, convenience stores, supermarkets, and gas stations. Students take *arubaito* to meet educational expenses and other sundry costs.

However, *arubaito* is not only undertaken by students; many Japanese people continue in part-time work even after graduation. These people are called *freeter*, an expression for people between the age of 15 and 34 who are unemployed or lack full-time employment, excepting housewives and students. The word *freeter* was first coined in the late 1980s, when the Japanese economy was booming, and is thought to be an amalgamation of the English word "free" and the German *Arbeiter* (worker). It originally referred to young people who refused to become permanent employees and instead engaged in temporary or part-time work. Also called "underemployed" or "freelance" workers, these are people who do not start a full-time career after graduation, and they tend to live with their parents and earn some money through low-paid and unstable *arubaito*.

The changing nuance of the *freeter* phenomenon is closely related to the development of the Japanese economy. The term *freeter* continued to be used during the economic recession which began in the early 1990s. During the bubble economy the term referred to young people who intentionally chose not to work full-time, but after the recession the number of full-time positions available for graduates radically decreased and increasing numbers of young people failed to find permanent employment, many choosing to accept temporary work instead.

In Japan, as in many other countries, the issue of a young generation which is not entering the regular labor market is becoming a serious social problem, and the term NEET, an acronym of "Not in Employment, Education or Training," has spread from the United Kingdom to Japan, South Korea, and China. Most *freeter*s or NEETs live with their parents and are financed by them. Social problems arise from this which are linked to the phenomenon of *hikikomori* (acute social withdrawal), this being one of the major social problems with which Japan is currently faced.

Another prevalent form of part-time work is *haken*, temporary work based on temporary contracts. Temporary work or temporary employment refers to a situation where the employee is expected to leave within a certain period of time. *haken sha-in* refers to contractual or seasonal employees, freelancers, or temps. They work for a certain company for a limited time based on the contract, rather than being life-time employees. People in Japan find *haken* work though the *haken-gaisha*, a temporary work agency, temp agency, or temporary staffing firm. Companies in need of short-term workers contract with the *haken-gaisha*, which retains temporary workers for the company with which it has a contract.

Japan is now seeing a dramatic increase in the number of companies seeking temporary instead of full-time workers. The increase in *haken* may also lead to social problems, because temporary workers have lower incomes, are not secure, and most importantly are not included in the national pension and benefits system. (H.C.)

See also: *shūshin koyō, seishain*

awase

合わせ

Adjusting to fit in

A shortened form of *suri-awase* (すり合わせ), which literally means "rubbing and putting together," in business contexts *awase* means combining ideas and opinions in order to reach a conclusion that works for all parties involved. The term originated in the practice of rubbing two finished edges of ceramic bowls together until they were smooth enough not to damage the lacquered tables on which they would be placed. The term is now used mostly within business situations and is often translated as "adjustment of views." The goal of *suri-awase* is to consult with the other party and find common ground pursuant to an agreement that satisfies all participants; *awase* by itself means "fitting in."

awase is ongoing in any business relationship. Whereas it might be thought that once *awase* is achieved the process of adjustment is over, the Japanese perceive that for any relationship to continue in the best and smoothest way possible, the parties must remember that change is constantly occurring. In order to maintain the best possible business relationship, *awase* is employed to help companies continue to grasp each other's changing ideas and needs.

Understanding of *suri-awase* can be essential to working with Japanese corporations. The American way of "beating out" trade agreements aims to arrive at an offer that will eventually make the counterpart see one's own way to the greatest degree possible. It is assumed in

Western dealings that one goes into negotiation with a preferred result or goal already in mind. This style of business is known in Japan as *erabi* (literally, "choosing"); such decisions are supposed to be made in as little time as possible consistent with achieving the desired result. By contrast, Japanese negotiating sessions may not be premised on the idea that two sides have already fixed upon certain goals, and tend to involve as many meetings and to go on for as long as it takes for the two sides to "rub" their ideas together until a mutually beneficial conclusion is reached. This process may take only a few days or could take months. There is usually less of a rush for decisions in the Japanese business world: Western companies can sometimes find this process tedious and inconclusive, whereas the Japanese sometimes find the *erabi* format abrupt and crude, and dislike what they consider the West's "either–or" attitude.

Still, a Japanese company itself may sometimes find this process too lengthy, and engage in *nemawashi* (literally, "to move a plant from one plot of earth to another"). In order to attempt to reach a conclusion without seeming too blunt or forceful, they might employ very subtle coercion, winning the other party over without their realizing it.

awase can also refer to the concept of anticipating what those around you desire, not just within meetings and negotiations, but with co-workers and others. It is important to understand what a person may want but is not saying; for example, a colleague who implies that you might want to take a break may in fact be saying that it is he or she who needs a break. Understanding unspoken messages is one of the most important parts of Japanese business and *suri-awase*. (T.C.)

See also: *kaigi, ishin denshin (chinmoku), eigo, hanseikai*

ba (genba)

場（現場）

Place

Adopted by Japanese systems theorists based on two Chinese characters—*gen*, referring to specific work, and *ba*, place—the term *genba* means "the actual place" or "the real place." Japanese detectives call a crime scene *genba*, and TV reporters may refer to themselves as reporting from the *genba*. In business, however, *genba* refers to the workplace, considered as the locus of creation of value: in manufacturing, the *genba* is the factory floor; in a therapy session or on the sales floor it is the place where the client meets the service provider; in a hotel it would be the reception desk or other places where the guest and staff come into contact.

In a broader sense, *genba* means the sites of the three major activities related to earning profits: developing, producing, and selling. Supporting the *genba* is one of the most important roles for management, since it concerns finding ways to make the company more successful and profitable, and the success of the company is seen as depending on how well it discharges this task. The *genba* walk, or "management by walking around," takes management to the front lines to look for waste and opportunities to practice *genba kaizen*. A systematic approach to improving processes (*kaizen*) requires managers to be attentive to the area where the action takes place. But although supervisors play a central role in *genba* management, workers too are also crucial: the needs of the *genba* can be more easily identified by the people who work within it, and people on the production line are always seeking solutions for problems or thinking about *kaizen* while they work.

The *genba* attitude reflects the idea that the reports, measures, and ideas transmitted to management are only an abstraction of what is actually going on in the *genba* to create value. Information about a process or what is happening in the *genba* is inevitably simplified and abstracted when reported, and this is often a reason why solutions designed away from actual processes seem inappropriate.

Imai (2007) sets out five "golden rules" of *genba*. First, if a problem arises, it is imperative to go to the *genba* first and not try to fix it via remotely. Second, one should check with *gembutsu* ("real thing"), meaning that when there is a problem concerning the *genba*, one should get as close as possible to that problem before proposing a solution. Third, provisional solutions are important, because even if the worker can't immediately solve a problem, it may be possible to mitigate it in the short term. Fourth, after resolving the problem the root causes must be identified. Fifth, once the problem is resolved the new processes must be standardized to prevent recurrence. For easy problems the "five whys" method may be sufficient, and although other problems require substantial preparation and planning, many can be solved on the spot and in real time. (M.E.)

See also: *genchi genbutsu, kaizen*

bengoshi

弁護士

Lawyer

A *bengoshi* is a person licensed to practice law in Japan as a lawyer or an attorney-at-law. The term is composed of three *kanji*, meaning to speak, protect, and serve. The lawyer is thus seen as playing a major role in the Japanese legal system, with the key functions of protecting human rights and ensuring social security.

bengoshi are regulated by the Practicing Attorney Law and unauthorized activity is prohibited. To qualify as a *bengoshi*, candidates have to graduate from law school, pass the bar examination, and do a one-year preparatory stint at the Legal Training and Research Institute of the Japanese Supreme Court. The qualification process is one of the most stringent in the world, with a pass rate of less than 3%.

After qualification, *bengoshi* join the Japan Federation of Bar Associations (JFBA) and a local bar association. Both organizations supervise the activities of the *bengoshi* and take disciplinary action against members who violate the Practicing Attorney Law. The JFBA guidelines provide basic rules on the duties of practicing attorneys. Loss of status, resulting in the *bengoshi* having to leave the association, is the most severe sanction.

Self-governance is an important concern for the JFBA and for the local bar associations. They must guarantee and maintain the independence of the *bengoshi* and the judicial system from the Japanese government. Toben, the Tokyo Bar Association, is one of the most important local bar associations and membership is mandatory for *bengoshi* who practice in the Tokyo metropolitan area.

It is possible for people without Japanese citizenship to take the bar examination. Attorneys from foreign countries who have the right to practice in Japan are called registered foreign lawyers (*gaikokuho jimu bengoshi* or 外国法事務弁護士). After approval by the Japanese Ministry of Justice, they can provide advice in legal matters which refer to the law of their home country. Registered foreign lawyers contribute to international arbitration issues in Japan but are not allowed to defend clients in a Japanese court.

bengoshi perform a wide range of activities. Most consider themselves generalists and maintain a broad knowledge of constitutional law, civil law, criminal law, commercial law, civil procedure law, and criminal procedure law. Besides traditional courtroom defense and argumentation, they provide legal services and advice, may be involved in governmental administration and legislation, and are able to serve as (part-time) judges. Solo practitioners are facing increasing competition from small and large joint offices, especially in urban areas.

As a result of the strict qualification procedures and the mandatory membership in the Japan Federation of Bar Associations and in a local bar association, the Japanese system of lawyers is often referred to as a guild or enclosed society. Loyalty and solidarity are strong among the bar associations.

It is notable that the ratio of lawyers to citizens in Japan is lower than in the other highly industrialized countries of Europe and North America. For business issues, legal problems are discussed out-of-court first, and there are relatively few lawsuits. In 2018, the number of practicing *bengoshi* stood at about 40,066, of which 412 were foreign-law attorneys. Female attorneys are playing an increasingly important role. However, the situation is currently in a state of change, because recent modifications to the examination process have increased the number of graduating attorneys. (M.F.)

See also: *chūkai, gai(koku)jin*

bentō

弁当

Lunch Box

The individual lunchbox, or *bentō*, is very common in the Japanese corporate world. It can be purchased in almost any food shop, with some fast-food restaurants specializing in it, and is a common meal for the Japanese worker on the go. It comes in a compartmented container and features several kinds of colorful foods. Although it is available at a wide range of prices (from cheap to gourmet), some families still carefully prepare their own *bentō* for days at work or school. If a *bentō* is purchased at a take-out restaurant, it is said to be a *hokaben* or *ほか弁* (named after the lunch box take-away service hokkahokkatei). More sophisticated *bentō* often featuring food shaped into comic figures are called *kyaraben* (*キャラ弁*).

Websites devoted to *bentō* have appeared as a new e-cooking trend, exchanging recipes, original ideas, and user-reviewed formulas. Several formats of *bentō* exist and trends continue to develop. The *bentō* has its equivalents in other Asian countries' cuisine and has become increasingly popular in Western countries as well. (Note: the honorific prefix *o* is often placed before the word depending on the context: thus *o-bentō*.)

The Kamakura period (1185-1333) saw the beginning of the *bentō*, which back then was essentially a bag with cooked, dried rice inside. Later, during the Momoyama period (1568-1600), boxes were used to pack lunches during cherry-blossom picnics. It was not until the Meiji period (1868-1912) that *bentō* started to be sold around towns and at train stations in the way they are today.

Chopsticks are generally included with the box if purchased at a take-out or may be matched to the box's color if prepared at home. The box itself may be decorated to appeal to the eater, whether it is with cartoon-like drawings (for children), pictures of popular icons (for teenagers and young adults), or traditional figures and pictures of beautiful women (for businessmen). If served in a fancy restaurant, the box could also be made of refined engraved wood; the outside of the box may be as aesthetically important as its content.

The types of food in a *bentō* are innumerable; virtually anything can be integrated so long as it is tasty, colorful, and harmonizes with the whole palette. The presentation of the food is crucial, and may even constitute a source of social advantage, for example for children who compare and trade their food at lunchtime in school. *bentō* have traditionally been used as gifts: a "love*bentō*," offered by a woman to a man, can express warm feelings. *bentō* can be served hot or cold and are sometimes re-heated. They usually feature one main compartment which holds rice or noodles and other compartments for side dishes. These other divisions complement the meal nutritionally, add flavor, and enrich the color scheme of the meal. These side dishes may include *tôfu*, noodles, omelettes, vegetables, pickled vegetables, fish, fruit, etc.

The type of bentō varies according to season and geographical location. A classic version is the *makunouchi-bentō* (幕の内弁当), featuring steamed rice topped with a pickled fruit, broiled fish, and an egg-based dish. The Chinese bentō (*chūka bentō* or 中華弁当) usually contains popular Sino-Japanese dishes. *tori-bentō* (鳥弁当) comes from the prefecture of Gunma and features chicken. The Japanese flag even found its way into the lunchbox, by means of the *hinomaru-bentō*, named after the "red circle over white" flag. The inside of the box consists of white steamed rice with a pickled fruit in the middle. (P.G.)

See also: *konbini, depāto*

bunkatsu hōshiki
分割方式
Divided Production System

bunkatsu literally means "split" or "division," and *hōshiki*, "method" or "form." The term has a rather general meaning, and is used, for example, in mathematics; but in the context of manufacturing it can best be translated as "divided production system," also referred to as cellular manufacturing or production. The divided production system is a form of lean management process that became popular in Japan during the late 1990s. In *bunkatsu hōshiki* the production process is divided up into small work units or cells, where each work unit executes multiple tasks, uses a variety of tools and equipment, and assembles products from start to finish. This reduces lag time for total production if problems arise in one of the units. *bunkatsu hōshiki* specifically refers to cellular manufacturing in which there are four to five workers in a unit performing a wide range of tasks. Most companies using *bunkatsu hōshiki* adopt the method as a transition phase towards two other cell production methods, *hitori hōshiki* (一人方式) and *junkai hōshiki* (巡回方式), which use one worker and two to three workers respectively and provide maximum line efficiency but with higher capital costs.

The *bunkatsu hōshiki* approach offers advantages to industries that need flexibility in production processes. In terms of human capital, workers are trained to do more tasks than those working in a traditional conveyor system. This makes workers more skilled and can reduce the number of employees needed for assembly. To further their skills, most companies will rotate their workers within each unit. This form of job rotation is known as *haichi tenkan* (配置転勤) and enables other unit members to help out where one worker faces problems. Having more skilled workers also increases the flexibility each worker has to respond to changes in production techniques and fluctuations in demand, since work cells can be rapidly modified and new products readily assembled, especially when no new equipment is required.

bunkatsu hōshiki has become a popular production strategy in Japan, especially in electronics, which is characterized by high demand fluctuation and consistent product improvements. Companies such as Sony and Toshiba have introduced cell production systems in their factories; in a recent survey, 70% of companies using cellular manufacturing said they were specifically using *bunkatsu hōshiki*, and more than half were planning on eventually adopting a *hitori* or *junkai hōshiki* system.

The goals of *bunkatsu hōshiki* are aligned with many of the goals of Just-In-Time (JIT) systems and other forms of lean management. Like JIT, *bunkatsu hōshiki* is designed to eliminate waste in production processes (*muda*). Implementing *bunkatsu hōshiki* minimizes production lag time, overproduction risk, and other unnecessary by-products involved in production.

There are close connections between *bunkatsu hōshiki* and certain *kaizen* philosophies. It is also interesting to note the similarities between *bunkatsu hōshiki* and the famous production assembly line system used by Toyota.

Although *bunkatsu hōshiki* is not the same as Toyota's system, it is fair to say that any Japanese company implementing *bunkatsu hōshiki* will have consulted with people affiliated with Toyota. (J.R.G.)

See also: *muda*, Just-in-time (JIT), *kaizen*

chōrei

朝礼

Morning prep-talk session

The practice of holding morning prep-talks, generally before the working day begins, is called *chōrei* (literally, "morning gathering"). These morning sessions are used frequently in Japanese companies, as well as in schools and other organizations.

The purpose of *chōrei* is to promote a spirit of unity and harmony (*wa* or 和) within the organization. A session often consists of reciting company mottos and/or singing company songs (*shaka* or 社歌), and helps workers to develop an emotional connection with their work. Additionally, the manager gives out information about the day's goals and provides any important information that may be needed. During *chōrei*, the manager will often encourage the workers to do their best (*ganbaru* or 頑張る), and to put in the effort to achieve the best possible result. The manager will also encourage workers to strive for continuous improvement (*kaizen* or 改善).

Every company will have a different approach to their *chōrei*. There are, however, common features. Typically, workers will all be dressed in company uniforms, and will seat themselves in the meeting room according to rank or status. They often begin with chants and perhaps songs. This is followed by speeches or lectures, often coming in quick succession with little or no pause between. Generally, there is no debate or discussion; at most, there will be one or two highly specific questions about the matter at hand.

The use of *chōrei* is an important cultural aspect of the Japanese workplace, and a unique aspect of Japanese management. It keeps everyone aware of important information needed to keep the workplace functioning efficiently—the manager can, for example, use the *chōrei* session to alert workers of problems with a particular machine and notify them of alternative procedures that are required for that day. But the benefits are not restricted to the obviously practical, since the *chōrei* also help to unify the workplace and create a bond between workers and the company. This is achieved because workers are being informed about relevant issues and kept in the loop, helping to bridge the gap between management and floor staff. Workers who are aware of a company's goals and strategies, and the potential obstacles, can identify with the desires of the managers and thus more likely to make efforts in the workplace and work harmoniously for the benefit of the company. This complements the group-orientation of Japanese culture. Whereas in Western society people value individualism and the pursuit of individual goals, Japan is very much the opposite, with heavy emphasis placed on working tirelessly for the benefit of the group.

chōrei complements the Japanese style of management. The traditional Western approach typically involves managers having their offices as far from the ground as possible, making them seem important, untouchable, and distant. Western managers traditionally have a distinctly different rank from the rest of the workers and are treated accordingly. Japanese management takes a different approach: managers often have offices on the ground floor, making them more accessible, and they place great emphasis on knowing the ins-and-outs of the business, frequently exploring the floor and speaking with the employees. They work with their employees rather than simply giving commands, and *chōrei* complements this by bringing workers and managers together, creating harmony and unity within the workplace, and removing the barrier of resentment between workers and bosses that is often found in the West. (C.G.)

See also: *ganbaru, shaka, wa, kaizen, madogiwazoku*

chūkai - chūkaisha
仲介 - 仲介者
Mediation, mediator

chūkai (mediation) is a quicker and more economical means of dispute settlement than arbitration or litigation. The parties to the dispute come together with the help of a neutral *chūkaisha* (mediator) who assists in the search for a resolution. Unlike arbitration and litigation, *chūkai* aims to arrive at an amicable settlement which satisfies all parties and does not depend on formal rules of procedure.

The role of the *chūkaisha* is to smooth communication and improve relationships between the parties, so that they can deal with each other again in the future. *chūkaisha* help the parties focus on the real issues of disagreement, and generate options that aim to meet the interests of all. They do not have authority to impose a solution; rather, their role is to reduce tension and remove obstacles in the way of a settlement. A wide range of people and institutions seek the aid of *chūkaisha*, including government agencies, corporations, schools, neighborhoods, community organizations, and even families.

Although Japan has long been known as a country that seeks to resolve problems with the least possible degree of friction, it does not have a long tradition of resolving disputes through mediation. Settlement-in-court and mediation were both introduced in the late 1800s, under the influence of the West. But while it is still popular in Japan to resolve problems through informal consultation without appeal to either judge or *chūkaisha*, the use of *chūkai* in business has increased since the 1980s. Successful court-connected mediation counts for approximately 55% of conflicts, and Japanese companies use mediation to make their business run more smoothly.

The Japan Commercial Arbitration Association (JCAA) provides mediation for any dispute which involves international transactions. It follows the rules and regulations contained in the International Commercial Mediation Rules and the Mediation Cost Regulations (JCAA). Most mediators are government employees. The government strongly supports court-connected mediation and provides court-connected mediators with the necessary education and training. Mediators appointed in connection to a court serve for a fixed period of two years, and afterwards may be reappointed by the Supreme Court for additional terms. The court-connected mediation system has both advantages and disadvantages. People who work as mediators come from various professions and are often retirees. Nearly 10% are lawyers or retired lawyers; there are also large numbers of female mediators, with many of the *chūkaisha* hired by family courts being housewives; and many others are elderly people who command great respect in their communities. This diversity of social and professional background is valuable, since mediators aim to incorporate common sense into the resolution of common disputes but can also be a cause of problems. (K.H.)

See also: *kaisha, ijime, shudan shugi*

daigaku

大学

University

The term *daigaku* refers to any kind of university, academy, or technical college. In ancient times the Japanese system of education was closely related to religion and Chinese Confucianism. In this period the purpose of *daigaku* was to teach public servants administrative skills such as accounting, to read and write in Chinese, and to understand the Confucian way of thinking including basic knowledge of astrology. Later, calligraphy, painting, poetry, and classical Chinese and Japanese literature became important subjects as well; but there was no system of final exams or graduation titles.

After the Meiji reformation in 1868 the education system changed. The European and especially the German system of education became a guide for all imperial universities, with the model of German Humboldt University being particularly influential.

After World War II the Japanese education system was again reorganized, shifting to a more American system with six years of elementary school, three years of junior high school, three years of high school, and—depending on the chosen university—two or four more years until graduation with a bachelor's degree. Some universities offer six-year programs leading to a professional master's degree. The two-year programs are limited to the *tanki daigaku* (短期大学) or *tandai* (短大), which are not really universities but colleges emphasizing study of home economics, nursing, teaching, humanities, and social sciences.

Japanese universities are organized in three different ways. They may be run by the Japanese state itself (national universities), the local province (public or local universities), or they may be private. In 2011 there were 780 universities in total, of which 86 were national, 95 public and 599 private. Famous national universities include the University of Tokyo, Kyoto University, and Osaka University; famous private universities include Waseda, Keio, Ritsumeikan, and Sophia. The total number of students is about 3.2 million.

Japanese universities are famous for their difficult entrance examinations (*nyūgakushiken* or 入学試験). Students who want to apply for a national university have to take two tests: first, a uniform achievement test set by the national government, and then an examination administered by the university itself. Applicants to a private university only take the university's examination: the more prestigious the university, the harder the test. The top universities are thus very difficult to get into and have many applicants. The entrance examinations are so hard that some applicants spend a whole year, during or after high school, at so-called *juku* or 塾 (from *gakushū juku* or cram schools) in the evening and at weekends. Sometimes high schools cooperate with specific universities to better prepare their students for the entrance examination.

After Japanese students have passed the entrance examination, it is often said that they then enter the best time of their lives. There is little pressure from examinations, as routine tests are quite easy, and students concentrate more on activities in circles and clubs (*bukatsu* or 部活), and enjoy their lives by having parties—perhaps for the first time, since university is often the students' earliest chance to escape the family households and live as an individual.

All universities have tuition fees, the amount depending on the fame or prestige of the institution. Students often have part-time jobs or *arubaito* to help their parents pay those fees as well as their own living expenses. Few students continue to study after obtaining a bachelor's degree. The next step is graduate school (*daigakuin* or 大学院), but as companies do not typically request students with advanced degrees, the motivation to keep studying—and so spend even more money and time on education—is very low.

To a Non-Japanese it may seem surprising that in the past, the class of graduation and field of study was not considered very important when students applied for jobs at a company. Job-hunting is very important to students, but the company paid more attention to the fame of the university than to faculty or grades. The fact that students attended a famous university often assured the company of their ability to learn, work hard, and push themselves (頑張る or *ganbaru*). Future employees had to show their loyalty by this spirit of *ganbaru*, especially if they were placed in a field which is not related to their former studies: in line with the mentality of learning by doing, new trainees learn everything on the job. This system is changing, since the

Keidanren has proposed new rules in hiring from 2020. Also, entrance examinations are bound to test diverse skills of prospective students from then on. (M.H.)

See also: *gakubatsu*, *sotsugyōshushoku katsudō*

danjo kōyō kikai kintō hō

男女雇用機会均等法

Equal Employment Opportunity Law

Discrimination against women has long been a prominent issue in Japanese human resource management. The *danjo kōyōkikai kintōhō* (Equal Employment Opportunity Law) was enacted in order to promote gender equality in employment. The first form of this law was *kinrō fujin fukushi hō* (Law for Welfare of Working Women or 勤労婦人服司法). This was amended to the Equal Employment Opportunity Law in 1985, and became effective the following year. The number of working women continued to increase, and the Equal Employment Opportunity Law was revised twice, in 1997 and 2006, to adjust to the changing situation. By establishing regulations for hiring and working conditions, the Equal Employment Opportunity Law aims as far as possible to treat both women and men equally. The law applies to full-time, part-time, and temporary jobs.

Japanese custom traditionally assigned men the superior position and expected women to be quiet and modest. Even after employment for women took off in the 1980s, the social status of women remained low and companies did not treat them as they did men. Women faced lower wages and had weak chances of promotion, amid claims that they were deficient compared to men. The Equal Employment Opportunity Law brought with it a new way of talking and thinking about roles at work. Women used to work as assistants and as secretarial support, with tasks such as copying materials and making tea, while work that actually involved doing business was reserved only for men. A program of positive action was therefore incorporated into the Equal Employment Opportunity Law. This program required companies to take measures to assist women in business—hiring more women, expanding the areas of responsibility open to them, and otherwise assuring gender equality.

However, the law has not always achieved its intended effects. Prejudices against women being equally able persisted and despite the raft of legislation intended to protect women's employment rights, the majority of company employees in higher positions were still men. With the new legislation, this classification of jobs according to gender became superseded by the terms *sōgōshoku* (management track or 総合職) and *ippanshoku* (administrative track or 一般職), the former meaning managerial jobs and the latter encompassing more general office work. Many women were encouraged to take the *ippanshoku* track right after they were hired, which never allowed them to reach management level and get higher salaries.

The role of the Equal Employment Opportunity Law is to create a workplace where everyone can work without unfairness. A serious issue in this connection is sexual harassment in the office. The first revision of the Equal Employment Opportunity Law (in 1997) dealt only with sexual harassment of women, while the 2007 revision expanded this to include harassment of men. The Ministry of Health, Labor, and Welfare runs an advice helpline in this respect. When a company detects behavior that can be considered sexual harassment, it is responsible for taking effective action to eliminate it. If the situation does not improve, the name of the company can be made public. The Equal Employment Opportunity Law also prohibits women from being forced out of a company in case of pregnancy. (KA.H.)

See also: *ippanshoku, sōgōshoku*

depāto

デパート

Department Stores

The name being an abbreviation of "department store," *depāto* (also referred to as *hyakkaten* or 百貨店) are retail chain establishments for apparel, specialty foods, and appliances.

There are notable differences between Japanese *depāto* and the typical Western department store: whereas the Western stores are often located in malls, *depāto* generally stand alone, and they may have many more floors or sections, offering a wide range of merchandise. The traditional *depāto* focuses on displays of mid-range to luxury brand apparel while also offering foreign exchange, travel reservations, and event tickets as some of their many services. Many have a *depa-chika* (department store basement or デパ地下) that caters as a grocery store and food court rolled into one, located on the lower floor level. While some Japanese go to the supermarket for their groceries, many also shop at the *depa-chika* for higher grade goods—American or Australian beef at a supermarket, but Kobe beef at a *depa-chika*. It is also very common for Japanese consumers to shop at a *depāto* for traditional gifts, in line with the Japanese culture's unique gift-giving customs.

The most prestigious and typically older *depāto*, such as Mitsukoshi, Takashimaya, Matsuzakaya, and Isetan, are considered symbols of cultural conservatism and sophistication, often with lavish displays of luxury brands in their display windows and on the first floor. Many *depāto* offer unique shopping bags which are commonly used by shoppers as a sign of status. But while many major *depāto* in Japan are nationwide or even international institutions, many are strictly regional. Each region (Hokkaido, Kanto, Chubu, Kansai, Shikoku, and Kyushu) has its own tailored and region-specific stores, such as Hankyu in Kansai or Tsuruya in Kyushu.

Although the Japanese *depāto* is under increasingly fierce competition from supermarkets, megamarts (such as Don Quixote), and *konbini* (convenience stores) in terms of accessibility and price, *depāto* continue to maintain their status in Japanese urban society as purveyors of quality, luxury, and status in both fashion and specialty items. If in the Western context the customer is "king," in Japan the customer is "god". Upon entering a store such as Takashimaya in Shinjuku, one receives a professional greeting from the exemplary staff. It is not uncommon for staff members to bow to every customer.

Some major Japanese *depāto* have sister branches with a specific consumer focus, and these are growing in popularity, especially with the younger generations. These specialty *depāto* are either fashion-oriented, such as Shibuya 109, Lumine, and Parco, or hobby-oriented, such as Loft or Tokyu Hands. Fashion-oriented *depāto* are havens for trend-loving youngsters, with boutiques crowded into a multi-level shopping mall focusing exclusively on apparel. Hobby-oriented *depāto* boast an extensive variety of "modern lifestyle" goods, such as homeware, sportsware, stationery, appliances, electronics, furniture, interior décor, etc.

Today *depāto* serve as shopping centers in the commercial focal points of large cities, located so as to better accommodate large volumes of customers. The *depāto* also have an historical link to the railway system, with many having been built by the private railway companies of the 1920s with a direct link to the stations themselves. The reasoning was that since so many Japanese people used the rail system as their main means of transportation (especially in Tokyo), building department stores alongside the stations would increase both convenience and sales volume. Typical examples of railway department stores include Atré and Tokyu Department Store, and it is common to find railway lines that have the same name as the *depāto* situated along them (for example, the Seibu *depāto* and the Seibu Shinjuku and Seibu Ikebukuro lines, the Keio *depāto* and the Keio Line). (W.H.)

See also: *konbini*

dōryō - dōkyūsei

同僚・同級生

Colleague, Fellow student

Although standard English–Japanese dictionaries render *dōryō* (同僚) as "colleague" or "co-worker," and *dōkyûsei* as "fellow student" in the world of Japanese business these two apparently unassuming terms have implications that run far deeper than their equivalents in the West.

A "colleague" in a Western business setting is usually someone who works in the same company or the same office building, regardless of position or age. While the term *dōryō* has a somewhat similar meaning, it is carefully calibrated according to the Japanese social system.

Japan has a strict hierarchical social system known as the *senpai* (or 先輩)–*kōhai* (or 後輩) relationship. When using the word *dōryō* in Japanese business, it is important to take into consideration the relationship to the "colleague" that is in question. In the *senpai–kōhai* system there are three basic classes into which a person can fall: *senpai* (senior), *kōhai* (junior), and *dōryō/dōkyūsei* (member of the same level). In this system, all *senpai* must be spoken to and referred to using the respectful language known as *keigo*. In Japanese business, a person's class or position is determined according to the date they entered the company; those who came before them are *senpai*, those coming after are *kōhai*. When using the word *dōryō* in a Japanese business setting, it is important to think of it in the context of someone who works in the same building of the same company and is of a class, grade, or position that is of similar nature. Although there are *senpai* and *kōhai* who can be referred to as a *dōryō*—that is, it is not only limited to *dōkyūsei* or members of the same class or age—the term cannot be used for someone who is a boss, manager, or of far superior status or position in the company.

Literally speaking, *dōkyūsei* refers to a person who is of the same graduating class as far as schooling is concerned. However, the word "classmate" does not capture the meaning of *dōkyūsei* as used in the Japanese business world, since it too has deeper implications. In the West a classmate is merely someone who graduates in the same year; *dōkyūsei* shares this core meaning, but it is also applicable to the relationship between a group of workers who enter into a company at the same time, making them "same year classmates" of that company. In a business setting, then, *dōkyūsei* translates as a "counterpart" within the company. The *dōkyūsei* is also a part of the "*senpai–kōhai* system." A *senpai* can use any kind of language in the presence of a *kōhai*, but a *kōhai* is always expected to use *keigo* towards a *senpai*. However, *dōkyūsei* are not required to refer to each other in *keigo*. Interaction between two members who are *dōkyūsei* is usually very equal: there is mutual respect and the language is relaxed. This interaction is the only place where there is complete equality between two people, as is usually expected in the West.

dōryō will most likely have similar positions and functions within their company, although there are also *dōryō* who become managers over their *dōryō* counterparts. In such a case, the language that is exchanged is still on the same level: *keigo* is not required nor expected.

In the Japanese business world, maintaining good relationships within a group is a very important virtue. Within the group, everyone strives to be unified, and relationships are thus formed that penetrate all class and status boundaries within a group or company. However, some of the closest and longest-lasting relationships that newcomers will form within a company are those with their colleagues or school mates from the same level. (K. I.)

See also: *senpai-kōhai, keigo, shudanshugi*

eigo

英語

English

The study of *eigo*—the English language—is a compulsory class from junior-high to high school and for at least one year in university. However, English is studied in the "cramming" style, simply in order to pass high school and university entrance examinations, and not as a communication tool. Thus, the Japanese sometimes lack experience of conversing in English and have strong feelings of denial toward speaking it in front of other people.

Since education until junior high school is compulsory, and English is a compulsory class throughout this time, all Japanese will have had at least three years' English education. The purpose of these classes is to learn about the English language and cultures, and to become able to communicate ideas in English. Nevertheless, because of the way in which they have been taught, many Japanese hesitate to use English. The frequency of English classes differs between schools, but they are usually held once a day or on every other day. In junior high, students learn basic English such as the alphabet, easy conversation, vocabulary, pronunciation, and translation between Japanese and English; but the main focus is on grammar. English classes continue in high school, but again these revolve around grammar.

Grammar is emphasized because the curriculum is organized so that students can attain high scores in high school and university entrance examinations. In the late

1970s, English education began to be seen as one of the principal subjects of compulsory education, together with Japanese and mathematics. The late 1970s were the heyday of the Japanese post-war economic miracle, and the period in which the ordeals of entrance examinations were at their most excessive. Students who passed the entrance examinations of famous high schools and universities had higher status; and although English was a means to passing those exams, and thus a gateway to further higher status, many Japanese had little experience actually communicating in it.

In business settings, English has become an important tool for communication with foreigners—a common requirement, since so many Japanese companies trade overseas. There is thus a need for workers who can speak English effectively; however, many have strongly negative feelings about the language which they associate with "cramming," and find it challenging to enter into discussions with foreigners. Even in an international business setting, many Japanese do not use English at all; when a speech in English is needed, the text is often prepared in advance and the speaker will simply read the manuscript aloud. Foreigners should be aware that most Japanese have difficulty communicating in English; learning some easy Japanese words will therefore be of great help in communicating, since it helps the Japanese to relax and so soothes the atmosphere.

Major companies have set up their own English teaching teams or allow workers to attend English conversation classes or language schools in their free time in order to raise the level of English in the firm. Furthermore, they are now encouraging the workers to get English qualifications for business trips, rewarding their efforts with promotion. One of Japan's major trading companies has required its workers to attain the score of 600 points or above in TOEIC, the Test of English for International Communication.

Although English is considered an important skill in Japanese business, many Japanese have difficulties expressing themselves because of the form of education they received. While the Japanese are trying to improve their English by educating workers, foreigners should bear this educational history in mind when they do business in Japan and realize that learning Japanese could pay dividends. (H.I.)

See also: *daigaku*

enryo

遠慮

Self-restraint

Self-restraint, or *enryo*, is a state of mind in which one politely declines an offer or an invitation, or refrains from doing something. It is considered a mannerly way to deal with situations that are inconvenient or unfavorable, allowing one to extricate oneself without causing humiliation or unnecessary stress for the parties involved.

enryo is a unique and essentially Japanese cultural characteristic. The difference between *enryo* and actually declining an offer is that a person who is *enryo*-ing may in fact want to do what is being offered. The true act of *enryo* is one that shows modesty and thoughtfulness towards the other person. No matter how tempting the offer, a Japanese person first declines it in order to show humility, which is considered a virtue of character. Therefore, in Japan, one should not always take "no" for an answer, at least not at first, for it could be an act of *enryo*. *enryo* is thus a form of courtesy, one of the techniques Japanese use to smooth interpersonal relationships. Because good interpersonal relationships are considered to be of great importance, it is important to know when and how to use *enryo* when communicating in Japan.

Suppose, for example, someone invites a Japanese person to come over to their home for dinner: the invitee almost always at first politely declines the offer, saying "Oh no, it's okay." This is not necessarily because he or she does not want to come; rather, it is *enryo*. After declining, the Japanese person will wait for the invitation to be offered again. If it is, this is a sign that the invitation is not just being given out of *tatemae* (front)—in other words, behavior that is expected by society or in particular circumstances. After being asked for a second time, it is acceptable to agree to the offer by saying *okotoba ni amaete* ("I will take you up on your kind offer"). Because of this complex and sometimes confusing characteristic of Japanese communication, it is considered safe for a person to show *enryo* first in order to avoid causing inconvenience or distress to the other person.

Japanese communication greatly relies on understanding. What a person says may or may not mean what the person is actually thinking; therefore, it is important to look for possible meanings behind what is being said. In order to tell the difference between what is said and what is implied, a person must understand the existence of *enryo*.

enryo does not only consist of declining an offer, such as a cup of coffee or a dinner invitation; not accepting praise is also considered *enryo*. For example, a Japanese person who is complimented on his outfit will not simply say "thank you," but will usually reply with something like *sonna koto nai desu* ("I don't think so") or *oseji ga umai* ("you flatter me"). These replies are an effort to show humbleness and self-deprecation and avoid appearing conceited or over-confident. However, because this is a form of *enryo*, one should not take those replies as dismissing the praise. When a Japanese responds to a compliment with *enryo*, this is regarded as a form of appreciation.

Japanese society values harmony and self-discipline, and *enryo* is also used politely to ask another person to refrain from doing something rather than issuing an order. For example, the phrase *kitsuen wa go-enryo kudasai* is heard or seen everywhere in Japan as a way of asking people to refrain from smoking. Directly asking someone to do something is sometimes considered rude, although when someone is asked to *go-enryo* it means the same as "do not." (R.K.)

See also: *amae, awase, giri, jōshiki, honne-tatemae*

gai(koku)jin

外（国）人

Foreigner

gaijin or *gaikokujin* are individuals from other countries who come to Japan either as visitors or as immigrants. In the context of modern-day Japanese management, the term refers to foreigners who work in Japan under a system in which they are treated as equal to their Japanese colleagues, with the same rights and social benefits. The term *gaijin* can seem somewhat offensive when used for foreigners, and often foreigners themselves do not like to be labeled as such, preferring to be recognized as a person from their home country.

The first foreigners to come to Japan were the Portuguese in 1542, numbers increased once Nagasaki was forced open to trade in 1859. As a result, more foreigners came to live in the foreign districts of Nagasaki, Kobe, and Yokohama. During the 1980s there was a large increase in foreign workers in Japan, likely due to the perceived economic benefits of the bubble economy. Linguistically, foreigners were first referred to as *ikokujin*, meaning different person of a different country, or *ihōjin*, meaning person with a different motherland. However, the term *gaijin* became predominant from the Meiji period onwards, referring to immigrants simply as "foreigners."

Japan is growing increasingly internationalized, and more foreigners are seeking to improve their lives through working for a Japanese firm. During the bubble economy period, many foreigners were seeking work and the companies themselves saw *gaijin* as a way to cut down on labor costs, opting to hire foreign workers over Japanese applicants. The money saved through employing *gaijin* allowed pay raises for lifetime employees within the company, and the Japanese companies also benefitted by not having to provide *gaijin* with equal rights within the company, including health care, insurance, and lifetime employment. Foreigners, just like part-time workers, could be fired at any moment.

In recent times this has changed. Japanese companies now make sure that foreigners put their college degrees to good use. Companies may have a two-year system where the *gaijin* attends a training program for about six months, and can then work full time for the remaining period. This program provides training for skills that may not have been provided by the academic degree, and in some cases Japanese language classes.

Japan is generally said to be an ethnically homogenous country, with the Japanese often being unaware of cultural differences and displaying certain stereotypes in their behaviors—ranging from the token blonde woman in a TV drama to the stares directed at foreigners on the streets and trains. The word *gaijin* itself tends to conjure images of individuals who are impatient, cannot speak Japanese or understand Japanese culture, and cannot fit into the mold of Japanese businessmen. But this is less true now than it was in the past. The myth of Japanese being a difficult language to learn is disappearing as more foreigners enter the workplace with a broad—albeit often imperfect—knowledge of

Japanese language and Japanese business practices. (E.K.)

See also: *eigo*

gakubatsu

学閥

Alumni of University

The English term "alumni" has the connotation of a graduate who continues to support their school or university by means most notably financial. The Japanese word *gakubatsu* is closely related to the English "alumni" (specifically, of a university), but with an importantly different shade of meaning. *gakubatsu* refers to a group of individuals who have graduated together, and in some cases can be used to describe a particular group or clique at or from a university. The emphasis in the term is on a circle of individuals who share a common ethos, one that is most frequently, though but not exclusively, seen among those who come from the same university. This concept is of particular importance in the business sector, where it has a place amid the repertoire of Japanese companies' employment methods.

Although the term *gakubatsu* reflects the nature of the Japanese university system, it also has a close connection with the concept of human relations (*ningen kankei* or 人間関係). Strong networks have historically been a powerful factor in the progress of Japan and are still evident in modern Japanese society. The idea of *gakubatsu* denotes a network of people who have shared experiences and enjoy a status that every member can recognize. It refers to individuals who belong to the same category, all members sharing the status of a graduate from their particular college or university. Given Japan's focus on *shudan shugi*— group orientation or 集団主義, rather than individualism—there is little surprise that *gakubatsu* are seamlessly incorporated into Japanese society.

One consequence of the existence of these *gakubatsu* groups is the formation of an unwritten ranking system. In her book *"The Japanese Society"*, renowned anthropologist Chie Nakane compares these *gakubatsu* networks to Indian caste groups, arguing that well-developed and sophisticated *gakubatsu*, coupled with the *amakudari* system, are core features of the controversial public–private sector relationship in Japan. Drawing on the model of the famous *gakubatsu* from the University of Tokyo (considered the top university in Japan), other universities have imitated this emphasis on group prestige—with four other elite schools (Kyoto, Hitotsubashi, Keio, Waseda) proving particularly successful in this respect, thus comprising what has become known as the "Big Five." This perpetuates the archaic yet still prevalent mindset that prestige and status are the most important facets of one's college and working career.

The recruitment and employment processes employed by Japanese companies assign a prominent role to *gakubatsu*. Many firms and organizations, in both the private and public sector, and including the Japanese government, have begun restricting recruitment to a select few universities (mostly the Big Five). The justification for this is two-fold. The traditionalist and prestige-conscious prospective employees reason that those who come from the same background will work in a more fluid and cohesive manner that will benefit the organization. This style of thinking had led companies to draw their labor pool from only one or two universities, to ensure that familiarity amongst new recruits will maximize the stability of the working unit. The other reason for unofficially instituting the *gakubatsu* recruitment system is the simple assumption that those who come from the most prestigious universities must surely be the smartest.

The escalation of the *gakubatsu* system has elicited negative reactions towards this highly restrictive method of seeking out future employment. What the *gakubatsu* system indirectly established was an understanding that the only course of success was to attend one of the top universities. This naturally generated tough and often stressful competition among students and families alike. Some companies disavowed the *gakubatsu* system entirely, claiming it to be blatantly corrupt. Soichiro Honda, of the Honda Motor Corporation is among those who openly opposed the system, describing *gakubatsu* as "the good old boy network," a reference to the American term for those who use their influence (usually financial or political) to help those of a similar social background.

While still partially in practice today, the *gakubatsu* system is slowly dissipating as businesses increasingly participate in a more globalized market economy. Many Japanese universities and companies are going through changes that even include the integration of some Western policies and customs. But although efforts are being made to minimize the effects of the *gakubatsu* system, the rank and prestige of the *alma mater* will always be used as a metric by companies looking to hire new recruits. (E.Kr.)

See also: *amakudari, sotsugyō, ningen kankei, shudan shugi, kaisha, fuhai, daigaku*

ganbaru - gaman

頑張る - 我慢

Achievement Orientation

It is very important in Japan to be orientated towards achievement. One of the highest virtues is that of doing one's best, persisting, and working hard. *ganbaru* is an active process wherein one works hard in pursuit of a goal, strives to overcome difficulties that might arise, and takes on difficult tasks even though they might be painful. It also embodies the philosophy of transforming one's own future and status by one's own efforts, and regardless of one's background.

ganbarism—a term formed from *ganbaru* with the English suffix "-ism"—is thought of as the spirit of *ganbaru*. This spirit can be applied to any kind of task: to sports competitions, studying for exams, or one's working life. The spirit of *ganbarism* is a fundamental part of Japanese society, which is learned at home and enhanced in the Japanese education system where hard study is necessary.

One of the most important places for Japanese students to *ganbaru* is in the university entrance exams. The students study long hours to get into a prestigious university, after which they are able to get a good job. Another case of *ganbaru* could be when a young adult leaves home from a small town for a big city. He must *ganbaru* to find employment, and then work hard so as not to disappoint his relatives back home.

ganbaru can be seen as deriving from early agricultural times when hard work was essential, and is supported by Confucian and Buddhist teachings which value work as part of life's fulfillment. The *ganbaru* spirit was also enhanced after the Meiji restoration in 1868, when status and social class structures were abolished, giving all Japanese people the opportunity to move forward. People then felt that it was possible to move up just by working hard; and the same sentiment can still be seen today, with everyone striving to advance regardless of social class.

In Japanese companies the *ganbaru* spirit encourages employees to work long, hard hours. In this case the *ganbaru* reflects a group obligation: one must work hard in order not to let the other team members down. Everybody in the workplace will cooperate to finish a difficult task, putting their personal lives on hold when faced with a deadline. This has a negative side: as well as working hard to achieve one's goals, *ganbaru* encourages employees to work without breaks or holidays. In a number of cases, families have demanded compensation for relatives who have died from overwork (*karōshi*).

Gaman is related to *ganbaru* but should not be confused with it. While *ganbaru* means actively working hard to overcome difficulties, *gaman* concerns the ability to patiently withstand something unpleasant that one has no power to change—a valuable character trait for Tokyo's cramped rush-hour trains.

Commonly used phrases include *ganbarimasu!*, which is said when one wills oneself to *ganbaru*; and *ganbatte!* or *ganbare!*, said to other people to urge and encourage them to work harder. (K.K.)

See also: *giri, karōshi*

genchi genbutsu

現地現物

"Go and see for yourself"

genchi genbutsu— "go and see for yourself"—has revolutionized Japanese firms and their business practices. This phrase encapsulates a simple but effective policy whereby employers immerse themselves in their company's daily operations and have direct knowledge of the production site (*genba* or 現場) or business section.

Information that circulates for too long can become simplistic and inaccurate. If a problem occurs, people are better able to understand and rectify it if they have ongoing and up-to-date knowledge of the site and the manufacturing process. *genchi genbutsu* is thus more concerned with empowering the individual to maintain the right mental connection with the workplace, rather than rewarding any specific actions they might carry out. Japanese managers believe that effective solutions derive from experience-based learning. By visiting a worksite and diagnosing a problem *in situ*, the employer will be able resolve it on the basis of personal experience and observations, rather than rely on accumulated data. *genchi genbutsu* is thus an effective management technique for improving processes and gaining experiential learning.

The nearest American equivalent to *genchi genbutsu* is "management by walking about," but the two approaches are importantly different. Western managers generally absorb and analyze information in a meeting, boardroom, or office, whereas in Japan this takes place on the factory floor. When a problem occurs, Western managers sit down at their desks to work out a solution, whereas a Japanese manager remains with the workers and is considerably more "hands on."

genchi genbutsu is one of the core principles of Toyota's famous production management system, and is completely integrated into Toyota's daily business practices. With certain notable employees embracing this policy beyond all expectations, Toyota's leading position clearly rests on the managers' willingness to engage directly with the production process.

When Yuji Yokoya, a Toyota engineer, had to redesign the Sienna minivan for North American consumers, he drove 53,000 miles around Canada, the United States, and Mexico in order to fully understand the needs of the American market. This drive encompassed many of the different types of terrain in north and south America. When crossing the Mississippi River, Yokoya noticed that the crosswind affected the stability; in Alaska there was a strong steering drift when driving on gravel roads; and the turning radius had to be tighter and more precise when driving through populated areas such as Santa Fe. Yokoya also wanted this vehicle to be family-friendly and to provide a livable environment for people who were spending a long period on the road. Yokoya's experience of American terrain fed through into specific design improvements. He could have read books which outlined the specifications needed, but elected instead to *genchi genbutsu*, in order to truly understand the North American consumers. As a result, sales for Toyota's

Sienna increased by 60%, car critics gave rave reviews to the newly improved 2004 model, and it became the second-best seller in the United States.

Even today Toyota still implements this practice. The "Toyota Five Continents Drive" in which Toyota engineers experience their product under very different and challenging conditions to improve the driving experience for their customers all over the world, is such an example. (S.K.)

See also: *ba (genba), kaisha*

gentei

限定

Limited Edition

gentei are special or exotic products, offered for a short period of time and in a limited quantity, and generally offered several times over the year as opposed to being restricted to a single release. The nearest English term would be "limited edition," but the primary motive for releasing *gentei* products in the Japanese market is not the novelty value, but to invigorate the market and stimulate interest in all of the products of the company in question. *gentei* are not core products of a company, and rely primarily on word-of-mouth for distribution; they are intended to be peculiar, and so to provoke discussions within consumer groups which in turn drives consumption of the company's mainstream brands.

Pepsi, for example, has introduced a wide range of branded soft drinks with exotic names and flavors—Ice Cucumber, Carnival, *shiso* (Perilla), White etc. Often these products are released for a very short period of time and are killed at the height of their popularity. The purpose of offering these limited lines is simply to attract the public's attention and boost the core Pepsi brand—in the very competitive Japanese soft drinks market, this is vital.

Similarly, popular confectionary KitKat has seen flavors including green tea, iced tea, apple, kiwifruit, cherry blossom, mango, soy sauce, pumpkin, and apple vinegar. This marketing approach is similar to Pepsi's, but KitKat has also released *gentei* based on wordplay: the word

"KitKat" being similar to the Japanese *kitto katsu* ("You will surely win"), a limited edition was produced aimed at high school finalists, resulting in a greater number of KitKats being brought to examinations. In addition, KitKat produces products for offer only in certain geographic regions, such as the potato option KitKat offered on the island of Hokkaido. These attract attention, are bought out of sheer curiosity, and act as souvenirs. (A.L.)

See also: *māketingu, shinhatsubai - shinshōhin*

giri

義理

Sense of obligation

giri refers to the set of ethical and moral principles which set out the ways in which one should fulfill one's obligations within society. There is no close equivalent term in English; although *giri* is variously translated as duty, moral and social obligation, and rules of social relationships, it is best understood as a combination of these meanings, and none alone can fully encapsulate it. It is a diffuse idea that permeates social relationships and interactions at every level; in modern Japanese society *giri* might manifest as a certain sense of obligation and debt toward someone for a service rendered, thus shaping the relations between "superior and subordinate, *senpai* and *kōhai*, parent and child, one owing a debt of gratitude he must fulfill to the possible extent of self-sacrificing devotion." *giri* also applies to business and work relationships, either between business partners or among co-workers.

giri originates from a set of unwritten principles regulating social life and cooperation in the villages of feudal Japan, which evolved into a more formal system with the advent of *bushidō*, the code of loyalty of the samurais. Here, *giri*, duty, took precedence over *ninjō*, personal feelings, and the samurai was expected to value his master more than his own life—much as long work hours are expected of the *salaryman*, to the exclusion of family life, and in exchange for material and social benefits. This conflict between *giri* and *ninjō* has been abundantly represented in traditional art forms as a painful moral dilemma, sustaining the idea that *giri* can indeed be a burden, incorporating a notion of sacrifice. The essence of the concept is still the same, although today's *giri* does not have the same strong connotations of subordination, or at least not to the same extent. Although *giri* is no longer formally implemented, it still has a pervasive and subtle influence on the way Japanese consider relationships. These principles are often misunderstood by Non-Japanese, since the ethic underlying them is based less on the concept of good and evil than on the promotion of group harmony and good relationships.

This duty to the group is strongly reflected in Japanese management, in keeping with the desire to promote strong human relationships—within the organization, as much as with external partners (the latter accounting, in part, for the notably long-term business relationships which Japanese companies tend to form). It manifests itself in the way one interacts with one's co-workers, *giri* encouraging a climate of mutual support rather than competition, with each trying to repay the other for any help provided. *giri* is also at the root of the strong links between *senpai* (先輩) and *kōhai* (後輩), and, in fact, for most relations of authority or support, even within a Japanese family. To a broader extent *giri* is also one of the foundations of the loyalty an employee shows towards an employer, since for a full-time employee who benefits from lifetime employment and the concomitant social advantages, the "contracted debt" is considered enormous. (J.L.)

See also: *senpai-kōhai, honne-tatemae*

goningumi

五人組

Quality Circle

In an effort to stamp out Christianity, the feudal authority in the Edo Period (1600-1867) created small social units, formed of five village households, in which responsibility for social conformity was diffused down to the individual members. These units, known as *goningumi*, have a modern counterpart in the Quality Circles favored by contemporary Japanese management. Quality Circles closely resemble the historical *goningumi*, both in their structure and the way they function.

The Quality Circle (earlier called a quality control circle) is a group usually of eight to ten people, from the same work area, who voluntarily engage in studying and solving product quality problems. In the Allied Occupation period, a statistical method of quality control was introduced by an American official from an office of the Supreme Commander for the Allied Powers. Under its influence, the Japanese government established the Japanese Union of Scientists and Engineers (JUSE), which worked towards launching a research and training program in 1946.

Strongly pushing the quality circle movement, the Japanese government passed the Industrial Standardization Law in 1949, and the Japanese Standards Association was founded. In April 1962, the magazine Gemba to Quality Control was published, and in May of the same year, the first quality control circle was registered at the headquarters of JUSE in Tokyo.

This officially signaled the beginning of the Quality Control Circle movement. In 1964 there were roughly 1,000 quality circles registered with JUSE, while in 1980 the figure became an astonishing 115,254 with almost 10 million workers involved. The first International Conference on Quality Circles was held in Japan in 1969. One impressive example of the quality circle in action involved cafeteria waitresses at a Matsushita plant; the quality circle of waitresses studied the different amount of tea for each cafeteria table and employees' behavior and was able to reduce tea-leaf consumption by half.

The development of the Quality Circles movement was driven not only by the circles themselves, but also through the input of government, companies, the law, and different organizations and associations. Quality Circles should not be confused with Total Quality Control (TQC): while the latter is a company's overall commitment to quality from product design and development to sales and after-sale services, Quality Circles are one prominent constituent of TQC, alongside many other crucial concepts.

Training plays an important role in quality circles. The circle leader is first trained by the senior management, and then devotes a remarkable amount of time and energy to disseminating statistical knowledge and other related expertise to his subordinates (either in work time or their own spare time). The consequence is greater worker participation and improved group dynamics, as every member is equipped with relevant knowledge and skills and can freely communicate his ideas. Thus, the existence of quality circles significantly improves product quality as well as productivity. Since suggestions given by circle members strongly stimulate innovation, and members (mostly engineers) are encouraged to register patents, the Quality Circle is also sometimes called the Creativity Circle.

In 1974, the Lockheed Missiles and Space Company in California became the first foreign company to adopt the practice of Quality Circles, with successful results. The number of Quality Circles, and QC consultants, subsequently mushroomed in Western countries. However, there is still a substantial degree of resistance to their use, with some believing that QC is an organic part of Japanese traditional culture and organizational practice—especially Lifetime Employment, which enables Japanese companies to train workers and invest for the future—and thus will not work in an equally effective and efficient way in Western companies. In support of their criticism, the detractors point to the hostile relationship between managers and workers, pressure from unions, and to the fact that there is no immediate (monetary) reward for these small group activities.

Critics of QC also say that this type of "bottom-up" management style may make decision-making overly time-consuming, which can have devastating consequences in an intensely competitive environment. Another criticism is that participation in the QC is not entirely of the workers' own free will, contrary to how the concept is usually "sold," especially in view of the fact that it is highly organized and institutionalized nationwide. Some even claim that the Quality Circle is paternalistic rather than participative, since there is no actual delegation of authority delegation to employees.

The Quality Circle is a hybrid of Western quality control methods and Japanese organizational practice, a grafting of feudal traditions onto a modern corporate structure. Despite the doubts and critiques, it is still rightly deemed one of the key factors behind the Japanese industrial miracle, and is properly seen as "uniquely" Japanese.

See also: *shudan shugi*

haichi tenkan

配置転換

Job rotation

haichi tenkan—job rotation—is the relocation of employees across different roles in a firm. This is a common and distinctive trait of Japanese management, practiced by over 60% of firms, with the proportion rising to 80% for the banking, finance, and insurance sector. Employees may be shifted to different positions, while managers are made responsible for different departments.

Through *haichi tenkan*, workers become familiar with the tasks of different departments; by thus increasing the flexibility of its workforce, the firm expands its potential to adjust to changing circumstances, gaining capacity to reconfigure its human resources according to the economic environment and so keep pace with the changing market—for example, the firm can shift excess labor to a department with excess demand. Besides the benefits at the level of the firm, *haichi tenkan* also allows employees to remain competitive. With technology changing rapidly, especially in Japan, job rotation allows workers to retrain and reskill while remaining within the firm; this can provide them with an effective form of insurance against the uncertainties of changing skill requirements in the wider market.

Dismissal of an employee is rare in Japan. Dismissal may be warranted when staff reductions are required and there is no possibility of *haichi tenkan* and *shukko* (transferring employees to a subsidiary or 出向); but, absent such extreme circumstances, *haichi tenkan* allows a firm to reallocate its staff rather than fire them. This is important in Japanese firms. Because of the practice of life-time employment, firms will contain many older or middle-aged employees, and *haichi tenkan* allows an inflow of new workers from different departments and an outflow of older ones, thus providing the benefits of displacement without the need to hire new employees or dismiss existing ones. Since the Japanese tend to stay in a single company for their whole lives, it is difficult for the company to bring in skilled workers from other firms; *haichi tenkan* therefore allows employees to share their skills with others.

The low unemployment rate is one of the factors behind the rapid growth of the Japanese economy, and in pursuit of this the government has supported *haichi tenkan*, providing subsidies and loans to those companies which provide internal training. However, although *haichi tenkan* is common, not everyone gets the chance to practice it. The scope for *haichi tenkan* depends on the industry and the size of the firm: the larger the firm, the higher the chance. Moreover, *haichi tenkan* is usually provided to full-time workers who are more educated, such as graduates. Retraining is costly, since time is needed for employees to adapt to their new environment and learn new skills, and other workers will need to spend time teaching them. So a company will generally provide more training to promising and valuable employees, and allow them to gain more comprehensive knowledge: the employees can thus contribute more to the company, and this in turn promotes loyalty. Unsurprisingly, it is the most valuable employees whose loyalty a firm most values. (T.L.)

See also: *jinzai kyōiku, tenshoku*

hanbei seido

販売制度

Retail System

Retail is the sale of goods and merchandise from a fixed location or through mail, for direct consumption by a purchaser who may be an individual or a business. Retailers are at the end of the supply chain, with manufacturers needing an efficient retail system as a part of their distribution processes. Retail establishments—shops and stores—can be located on streets, in residential areas, or in shopping malls and department stores. Non-shop retailing uses the Internet or mobile phones as a tool for electronic consumption, mainly for business-to-consumer transactions as well as for personal mail orders.

Japanese business is distinguished by its emphasis on building long-term relationships between partners, providing top-quality customer service, and the unique role of retail establishments; these characteristics are underpinned by a retail distribution system—*hanbei seido*—which is often viewed as one of the world's most complex and extensive supply networks. Multiple layers of manufacturers, importers, retailers, and wholesalers combine to form an extensive distribution web, within which, because of the Japanese people's innate cultural sensitivity to relationships, businesses prioritize personal relations with partners over logistics and the results of negotiations.

The modern Japanese retail system has its roots in the distribution systems characteristic of the Edo Period.

Then, Japan was divided into self-contained regions connected through complex allocation systems to ensure the efficient distribution of goods. From this foundation, the modern Japanese retail system has evolved to incorporate numerous intermediaries.

With the growing employment rate following World War II, the rate of formation of retail shops increased, further strengthening the relationships between manufacturers and retailers. Intimate relationships are the basis for business interactions, and enhance communication across numerous channels due to the close associations between intermediates. Loyalty also promotes mutual cooperation within the group, lessening the degree of competition. These positive relationships develop in parallel with the dedication to ensure the highest quality of customer service. A characteristic of Japanese stores is that shops are often willing to deliver directly to the customer's house. *takkyubin* （宅急便）is a national delivery service transporting various packages directly to consumers' homes, and their prompt delivery and modest costs have enabled the Yamato Transport Company to remain the leader in personal delivery services.

Wholesalers play a significant role in storing, distributing, and marketing goods to regions within and outside of Japan. Wholesalers are themselves multifaceted, and products pass through many wholesalers before finally reaching the retailer, something which results in inflated prices. Retailers will also sell products back to the wholesaler, particularly in the clothing industry. Most returned goods will have been bought by the seller under purchase contracts, but are accepted back by the wholesaler under customary law. Wholesalers in Japan will often deliver shipments directly to a retailer, and to reduce the risk of unsold products and costs of storing inventory, the wholesalers tend to supply smaller quantities at a time.

With the increase in price sensitivity and demand for cheaper products amongst consumers following the economic crisis of the 1990s, the traditional distribution methods are now facing challenges to their established model of a complex retail system involving many intermediate suppliers. Trends have developed towards new supply chain models and backward integration; Uniqlo, for example, has begun to both produce and retail its own products. Low-price distribution channels, including discount and convenience stores, have emerged as more convenient and cost-efficient channels of consumption while also providing for lower production costs. Convenience stores like 7-Eleven, Lawson, and Family Mart have adapted to the needs of the Japanese people and engendered a revolution in the process—long hours, accessible in residential areas and around train stations, these chains offer a variety of products and services which exemplify the "convenience" of these types of stores and so differentiate them from supermarkets or department stores. (P.L.)

See also: *konbini, depāto, ningen kankei, māketingu, shitauke*

hanseikai

反省会

Reflection meeting

A compound of *han*— "change" or "turn over"—,*sei*— "review" or "examine oneself" and *kai*—"meeting"— *hanseikai* is the term for a reflective meeting and refers to the Japanese practice of reflecting as a group on what has been done, which is not only an intellectual exercise but also intended as a thoughtful and even poignant experience. It usually consists of three components: realizing that there is a gap between expectations and achievements; taking personal responsibility and being open to negative feedback; and committing to a particular method to overcome the problem. Inside a company, *hanseikai* are intended as reviews of what went wrong in a project, regardless of whether or not the project was successful. Its basis is that it is not enough just to realize your weaknesses: one must also be able to change and fix those weaknesses.

hansei or "reflection" about work is part of a larger process that takes place in Japanese companies, known as organizational learning, in which a system is created to constantly educate the firm's employees. Organizational learning consists of four stages: planning, acting, reflecting, and memorizing. *hansei* would correspond to the third stage; thus, workers will first outline the desired achievement, then try to reach it as planned, and later conduct the *hanseikai*. Here, members of the company will exchange feedback, examine what they have done and whether it follows the company's practices, and analyze whether everything has been done correctly. The final stage consists of transmitting the information to other members.

hansei is not only practiced in companies, but is widespread in Japanese culture. It is a practice that is highly esteemed and valued. *hanseikai* are even held in schools: from an early age, the teacher will gather the students together after class to ask them how the day went, if they did well and if they could have performed better. This trains Japanese people from an early age to be self-critical and willing to analyze their actions and accept advice. In Japan, self-criticism, as well as the ability to request and gratefully accept criticism from others, is a sign of competence. Criticism will usually be directed toward the group rather than an individual, with the intention of improving the group as a whole rather than just one member.

hanseikai focuses on what went wrong during a process and so devises new plans intended to ensure that those mistakes do not recur. Thus, *hanseikai* meetings are held frequently, criticizing and objectively evaluating the topic of discussion for the purpose of improving it. The *hansei*, or reflection, is a type of mindset, and can range from a quick pondering over what was done to a deep and honest assessment of performance and results. The reflection can also be directed toward oneself.

hanseikai are also held in *goningumi* or quality circles. *goningumi* are formed by blue-collar workers within a company who will choose a firm-related topic and try to improve upon it. Since they mainly seek self-improvement and are not a mandatory managerial practice, the self-motivation within these circles is very high. All of this aids constant and successful organizational learning.

Many Japanese companies are very strict about taking the time to hold *hanseikai* after finishing a project or after a day's work—Toyota is a prominent example. This need to constantly improve in order to achieve perfection is characteristic of Japanese culture. This is known as *kaizen*, a Japanese management practice that looks incessantly for superior performance within the company. *hanseikai* can be seen as the basis of *kaizen*, the objective being not to hurt the individual but rather help him improve. (C.M.)

See also: *goningumi, kaizen*

heijunka

平準化

Leveling out production

The suffix -*ka*, added to a word, confers the sense of "change"; when added to the word *heijun* (level) the resulting term *heijunka* thus means "levelling," "making something level," or "making something equal or uniform. *heijunka* is most commonly used in reference to production. Production can be leveled in two ways, through type and through quantity (of products).

The concept of *heijunka* can best be summarized with a short example: Suppose a company manufactures two cars, type A and type B, and their production schedule is as follows:

Before *heijunka*

Week 1: AAAAAAAA

Week 2: BBBB

Thus in week 1 the company produces 8 cars of type A, and in week 2,4 cars of type B.

After *heijunka*

Week 1: AABAAB

Week 2: AABAAB

Thus, in both week 1 and week 2, the company produces 4 cars of type A

and 2 cars of type B.

In this example, *heijunka* has leveled the type (by producing the same types in sequence each week) and also the quantity (by producing the same quantity each week). The total orders for this two-week period were 8 cars of type A and 4 cars of type B or 12 cars in total.

To level the type, find the ratio of the products being produced. The ratio of 8 of type A and 4 of type B is 2:1. So for every 2 cars of type A that are produced, 1 type B should be produced. To level the quantity, take the total number of orders and distribute them evenly over the time period. There were a total of 12 cars in this two-week example, so each week there should be 6 cars produced.

Traditionally, many companies think that producing a large batch of one product at a time is favorable. Why? Because in this way it is possible to get a bulk discount on raw materials and spend less time involved in changeovers from producing product A to producing B. For many managers, saving money (by ordering in bulk) and saving time (by avoiding changeovers) constitute sufficient reason for producing in this style: however, there are many down-sides to this approach.

(a) Longer lead times are required: if there is a demand for a certain product that is not currently in production, a customer will have to wait until production switches to the model they are looking for. With *heijunka*, production is constantly alternating between the different types, ensuring a constant flow of all products.

(b) Larger inventories are needed: if a company is producing products in large batches, there will be a need for a large work-in-progress inventory as regards raw materials, and also a large inventory of identical finished products at the end of the batch. With *heijunka*, the variety of products produced in a cycle is closer to the rhythm of actual demand—in other words, on any given day sales are more likely to be spread thinly across various products, rather than concentrated on one.

(c) Quality may be put at risk: if there is a batch-wide defect in a product, enormous losses will be incurred fixing/discarding all the defective items. With *heijunka*, defects are more likely to reach the market and be noticed before a large quantity has been produced.

(d) Workers may become inefficient: in producing different batches every day, workers will have different amounts of daily work. Some will be busy, some not. This can lead to tensions, and thus to lower morale and less regard to safety. With *heijunka*, the work is more evenly spread, and everyone performs his/her share each day, leaving less room for this tension to build up.

(e) While it is true that when ordering in bulk it is possible to get a discount from a supplier of raw materials, these large sporadic orders may not always be capable of being fulfilled. With *heijunka*, on the suppliers' side there is constant and consistent demand from a company for parts, which means the supplier can also hold less inventory and plan their operations with more precision. This is a chain reaction that translates into reduced prices for everyone, including the customer.

Having said the above, *heijunka* isn't perfect. While *heijunka* can cut down on lead time, the company must have a fairly good estimate of customer demand. The company may prefer to have customers place their orders for something first, and then wait for the duration of the production process before they receive their product.

As one of the fourteen principles of the Toyota Way, *heijunka* is a response to the three wastes—*muda*, *muri*, and *mura*. *heijunka* is a direct response to *mura*, but by correcting this, *muda* and *muri* are also affected. In a standard production line the items produced from day to day usually vary (*mura*). This means that there will be some days when the employees and the equipment are overworked (*muri*). If the employees are overworked, they may be more apt to overlook safety and quality issues; if the machines are overworked, they are more likely to break down or start introducing defects (*muda*). The purpose of *heijunka* is to efficiently eliminate these three wastes. (R. M.)

See also: *muda-muri-mura*

hiragana - katakana

平仮名 - 片仮名

Japanese Alphabets

hiragana and *katakana* are the two sets of modern Japanese alphabets. In the modern Japanese writing system, the two *kana* (仮名) scripts are used in a combination with *kanji* (漢字), or the Chinese characters. *hiragana* and *katakana* have different roles and usages in expressing Japanese words. In contrast to the logographic *kanji, hiragana* and *katakana* are syllabic.

In the past, the Chinese characters were used for phonetic purposes to meet grammatical requirements, known as *manyogana* (万葉仮名). Starting in the late 8th century, *manyogana* began to be simplified and the simplified forms appeared in written documents. For example, the *Tale of Genji* made extensive use of simplified *manyogana*. The simplification continued and *manyogana* gradually transformed into the modern *hiragana* and *katakana* forms. In 1900, *hiragana* and *katakana* were standardized by the government and began to be taught in elementary schools. The Japanese writing system underwent a further reform after World War II, thus introducing the current Japanese writing system.

hiragana and *katakana* are both syllabaries, meaning each character represents a syllable. There are 46 *hiragana* and 46 *katakana* characters in the Japanese language, in which one *hiragana* and one *katakana* character correspond to the same syllable. Basic Japanese syllables are constructed with 5 vowels and 9 consonants. A syllable can be a vowel only, a consonant followed by a vowel, or a consonant only. In addition, there are several modifications that can be made to certain characters in order to express more syllables. For example, adding two dots called *dakuten* (濁点) to *ha* (は) will change it to *ba* (ば).

The two *kana* scripts serve critical roles in the modern Japanese language, and can be distinguished according to their different usages. *hiragana* are the primary Japanese alphabets, and are used for grammatical endings, grammatical particles, as a reading aid for difficult *kanji*, Japanese words without *kanji*, Japanese words with *kanji* that are difficult to read or not known to an ordinary reader, and for Japanese words that are too formal to write in *kanji*. On the other hand, *katakana* is mainly used for foreign-derived words—known as *gairaigo* (外来語)—including personal names, names of foreign places, and technical or scientific words. Other usages of *katakana* include onomatopoeia, interjections, and common animals, plants, or objects whose *kanji* are uncommonly used. (S.M.)

See also: *kanji*

honne - tatemae

本音・立前

Public Face and Private Face

tatemae, which can be translated as "front" or "facade," is the face that the Japanese show in public. People may have specific roles due to their social status or position in a corporation or company; in their roles, they behave as they are expected to behave, regardless of their personal opinions about the matters in question. The core of *tatemae* is politeness so as to avoid confrontation. In Japanese society, especially in the professional field, there is always a double social reality, described by means of two words whose meanings are diametrically opposed: *tatemae* (official, public, socially required reality) and *honne* (informal, personal reality which disregards social parameters; a literal translation might be "real intention" or "genuine truth"). Outsiders might think of Japanese society as being honest about casual dishonesty; however, for the Japanese themselves it is more like an acknowledgment that there is more than one mode of honesty.

The scope of these two words is not limited to social interactions. In purely factual discussions such as on the news, or as regards politics or the economy, there is room for *tatemae* and *honne* to run in parallel, providing a safe way to contemplate sensitive issues. The fact that the difference between these two modes is made explicit in Japanese can be seen as an indication that the Japanese are "honestly dishonest"; yet it can also be seen as a mark of a people that values true sincerity so much that it makes its insincere moments explicit, thereby implicitly apologizing for them.

This solidarity in effect enables the population to support each other, to cheer each other on, and to feel that they are not alone in any task they may undertake. Society is there to help those unfortunates who may get lost along the way. However, this solidarity has a price. If the expression of feelings is prohibited and everything is focused on unity of thought, the resulting tension can be difficult to manage. Unless ways are found to release this tension from time to time, the consequences of this pressure can be terrible. This is the reason why *nomikai* (drinking sessions with one's colleagues or 飲み会) have become a sort of necessary respite. *nomikai* become a privileged place where one can freely express opinions. (M.T.)

See also: *uchi-soto, giri/ninjō, nomikai*

hoshin kanri

方針管理

Goal setting, implementing strategy

hoshin kanri can be translated as strategy or policy deployment. It is a Japanese business term describing a method for finding and pursuing long-term strategies or visions, where the objective is to improve the performance of the whole company by improving cooperation between every department therein, and by using human resources as efficiently as possible.

As a first step of *hoshin kanri*, the top management of a company develops long-term visions. A vision can, for example, be that a firm should achieve more flexibility on the production line in order to better meet the clients' demands without increasing costs.

The next step is to translate this vision into short-term goals and find concrete measures to achieve them. In *hoshin kanri*, the vision cascades down through the company hierarchy, starting from the top. Teams on every level split this vision into smaller, more concrete goals and think of strategies to achieve them. For example, the development division thinks about small but cheap adjustments in response to clients' demands, the production department tries to optimize the process of producing different products on the same production line, while the sales division tries to gather information about the clients and also tries to reduce the costs of storage and delivery. Within each department, those goals are now given to different offices on the next lower level of the hierarchy, teams in every office further concretize the goals, and so on.

The important difference from similar processes in Western firms is that each department gets only general instructions and decides on its own how to make those more concrete. As long as the vision is met, top management doesn't intervene. Often processes like *kaizen* or continuous improvement are used in order to achieve the goals.

This method works especially well in Japanese firms, since the top management takes a more passive role than in the West. In a Japanese company, many decisions are made through bottom-up processes, better fitting the Japanese mentality of harmony and group-orientation. The top management gives its consent to decisions made at lower levels and tries to harmonize them.

In a Western firm, the management tends to give more precise orders and tries to control every important decision within the company. Thus it can thus find it difficult to adopt *hoshin kanri*, since the employees are not used to being integrated into the process of defining goals and developing strategies. Nevertheless, there have been several intriguing attempts to adapt *hoshin kanri* to the West.

A strength of *hoshin kanri* is that long-term visions can be translated into short-term goals rather easily. This allows companies to develop visions and to pursue them, instead of concentrating all their energy on everyday activity. Another advantage is that it is possible to utilize the human resources of every level more efficiently, since everyone is integrated in developing goals and strategies. A side-effect is that employees who feel integrated and acknowledged will normally be better motivated and so perform better.

hoshin kanri also helps to reduce the inefficiency that occurs due to rivalry and conflicts between different departments, since it reduces the competitiveness of the environment. But there are also disadvantages. In order to develop goals or strategies, every department or office needs time for group meetings. Since many people are involved in the processes, this can take a long time and radical changes are very unlikely. However, although this can lead to increasing costs, Japanese corporations believe these initial expenditures will pay off in the long term. (M.M.)

See also: *goningumi, kaizen (genba kaizen), shudan shugi (kojin shugi)*

iitokodori

いいとこ取り

Adopting aspects of foreign cultures

One of the secrets of Japanese business success is *iitokodori*—picking the best of everything, and incorporating the strengths of others' practices while avoiding the drawbacks. In management, this equates to adopting the best of foreign imports; but *iitokodori* is not simply a management technique, but can best be described as a positive approach to creating value for Japan overall, making the culture richer, living easier, and the citizens more satisfied.

The idea of *iitokodori* took shape during the Meiji Restoration, as Japan sought to catch up with and overtake the technological culture of the West. To do this, the Japanese had to be flexible enough to adopt aspects of Western culture according to their taste. One thing to do was to change eating habits, leading to the introduction of *yōshoku* (洋食)—dishes imported from Europe or America but shaped in true Japanese fashion and cooked to fit local tastes. Here there are great examples of *iitokodori*, including a Japanese-style hamburger, with Japanese seasoning and no bread.

Culture-enriching *iitokodori* is carried out in many other areas as well. One example is the construction of the Japanese language itself, which was adapted from the Chinese writing system. Japanese took the characters and changed them by reworking and simplifying them to suit their own grammar and writing system. The result was *hiragana* and *katakana*, and through *iitokodori* these systems merged into the present system over the centuries.

Understanding foreign cultures eventually affected Japan's ability to innovate for the global market. Thus, *iitokodori* is also an important factor that led to the rise of the nation's economic power. The openness to the outside world brought about a better-educated labor force, leading Japan to become great innovators such as in developing new technologies and refining designs. Japan is now known as a major technology exporter, symbolized by flagships such as Toyota and Sony.

Japan made itself wealthy by adopting and adapting other cultures' technology and institutions. Nowadays, *iitokodori* is not just seen between cultures or firms, but is also present in people's daily lives—in conversations, projects, or even in one's identity. An example of the latter would be taking on the look or personality of someone one admires, and combining it with the best aspects of oneself in order to become a better person. Thus, even one's own thoughts and ideas can be the subject of *iitokodori*.

Iitokodori is successful specifically because the Japanese are always open to new ideas. The culture is constantly looking for, researching, and welcoming advancement in diverse fields. The Japanese like new resources and want to use the good ones as a tool to make their culture better. As a matter of fact, the fundamental purpose of *iitokodori* for the Japanese may simply be to develop and maintain the best possible culture, not only for their own sake, but also for the rest of the world. (Y.N.)

See also: *burando ryoku, kaizen, shikata*

ijime

苛め

Harassment

ijime translates as "bullying" when it occurs in schools and as "harassment" in the workplace. In both realms, it has become a social issue. Until recently *ijime* was largely taboo, but as attention from the mass media has brought it more into the light, it has become clear that many people have experienced it.

At workplaces, *ijime* can lead to employees quitting their job; to depression, stress and suicide; or even simple social awkwardness such as is associated with being left out of the group. The conflicts which may trigger it can be relatively small—perhaps someone wants to work overtime while others want annual leave—but when handled inappropriately they trigger *ijime*. *ijime* can manifest as people having to work on shifts that nobody else wants to work, having to work overtime without payment, not being invited to a group meeting, or even not being giving any work at all. As harassment continues over time, people gradually become humiliated, intimidated, frightened, and may eventually resign.

According to a government survey from 2016 30% of respondents reported power harassment, and complaints to labor bureaus rose from 22,153 in 2006 to 70,917 in 2016. The power harassments include being shouted at, threatened, and scolded, or being shunned by co-workers. The survey further showed that 85% of these cases of *ijime* occurred between superior and subordinate.

For many years there was no law preventing power harassment in Japanese firms. In early 2019 the Japanese government developed a draft bill that requires companies to prevent abuses of power. In the event of this draft becoming a law Japanese companies will have to take serious measures to prevent abuses of power and protect their employees from power harassment. (H.N.)

See also: *chūkai, chūkaisha, senpai/kōhai*

ishin denshin – chinmoku

以心伝心 · 沈黙

Communication without words

ishin denshin is a Japanese concept for a condition when two individuals are able to reach a mutual understanding without the use of words. Individuals are able express their feelings and desires through the use of body language, facial expressions, and other nonverbal signs. Meaning "heart-to-heart communication," *ishin denshin* is more a symbolization of the Japanese attitude towards human communication than an attainable state.

inshin denshin is of specific importance in Japanese management, where it highlights the main difference between Western and Japanese communication; whereas the Western approach stresses direct speech and conciseness, its Japanese counterpart tends to look poorly on such a direct and upfront approach. Concepts such as *chinmoku*, literally meaning "silence," and *haragei*, translated as "body language," also play an important role in the development of *ishin denshin*. Generally, *ishin denshin* can be considered a state of "mental telepathy" between two individuals, which is very important when considering the Japanese concepts of *honne* and *tatemae*, the difference between informal and formal communication.

In general, direct speech in Japanese society and management is not popular and carries negative connotations. To express one's thoughts before a group in the absence of an actual consensus is considered to be selfish and rude. Furthermore, such an open display of personal opinion carries the stigma of being thoughtless, impolite, and immature. In order to preserve social harmony, Japanese communication thus has a strong preference for the idea of *ishin denshin*.

As a result of this preference, *chinmoku* is often displayed within the workplace as a form of respect. Strongly influenced by Zen Buddhism traditions, *chinmoku* has gained significant importance as a method of self-restraint and consideration. Since group consensus plays a much larger factor in Japanese management, the act of remaining silent and withholding one's opinion or idea is seen as appropriate.

Generally, *chinmoku* is a method is in which social harmony (*wa*) is preserved. Since personal opinions may seem to be selfish or even offensive in cases, silence is seen as a better alternative. However, the concept of *chinmoku* deeply contrasts with Western philosophy, where silence is viewed as a sign of a lack of opinion rather than a form of self-restraint.

Another concept that complements *ishin denshin* is *haragei*. Loosely defined as a technique that allows an individual to express their emotion without verbal actions, *haragei* is closely associated with *ishin denshin*. However, the two concepts are very different and should not be confused; whereas *haragei* refers to the actions and methods employed to express intentions non-verbally, *ishin denshin* is the state or condition in which verbal communication is no longer required in order to convey messages.

ishin denshin is not achieved in the workplace, but through the accumulation of social events such as *nomikai*s where individuals are free to express their *honne*, or inner feelings. Social events play an important role in the development of *ishin denshin* because individuals are often forced to display *tatemae*, or submission to societal obligations, and therefore are not able to express their true thoughts. As such, *ishin denshin* is necessary in order to understand and effectively communicate within the workplace.

For the sake of social harmony and preservation of the group consciousness, *ishin denshin* has come to play an important role within Japanese communication. Since direct speech and individualism is strongly discouraged, alongside the practice of *tatemae* in the workplace, *ishin denshin* serves as a means to effectively communicate without having to disrupt the social balance. (S.N.)

See also: *honne - tatemae, nomikai*

jidōka

自動化

Built-in-Quality

jidōka—"automated"—refers to the automated procedures which Japanese manufacturing companies expect from their workers on assembly lines. As such, *jidōka* represents the smooth, on-time, cost-effective, and methodological process of production—in which goods are faultless and exactly the same—which is characteristic of Japan. Although this may seem similar to the expectations of assembly lines anywhere else in the world, Japan pays especial attention to details and the use of relentless energy to achieve a standard of product or service that is second to none.

jidōka places people in an exact position so they can be responsible for a specific part of a product. They follow very precise procedures so that everything works consistently from one step to another. The advantage of this is that customers have a clear view of what they can expect, and the high expected standards are maintained. But the disadvantage is that the process struggles to find the flexibility which permits product differentiation.

Great Japanese firms such as Toyota are firm believers in *jidōka*, which for them goes hand-in-hand with Just-in-Time management. Toyota understands *jidōka* as having two parts:

1. Quality Maintenance. Each manufacturing section is equipped with automatic detectors that can detect when a product is abnormal and automatically switch off the entire procedure; and alongside this each individual

worker has responsibility for quality checks for their specific sectors and must report immediately when abnormality is manually detected.

2. Decreasing Number of Workers. If *jidōka* occurs as mentioned above, then there will be less need for many workers to be assigned to a sector. Thus, workers can be reassigned. As a result, a single person can be put in charge of several machines, lowering labor costs as well as smoothing the process of production. The work that can be done by machines will no longer be done by manual workers, and manual workers will only be asked to do jobs that are too complicated for machines. This form of labor division is not only cost-effective for the company but will increase the rate of production, further satisfying the needs of Just-in-Time production.

As with any production line system, *jidōka* represents monotonous work which leaves people doing the same thing continuously, relying heavily on automated systems. To mitigate this, Japanese management has developed several auxiliary techniques such as *bunkatsu hōshiki*, *goningumi*, and *haichi tenkan*. (N.Y.)

See also: Just-in-time (JIT), *gonin gumi*, *haichi tenkan*, *bunkatsu hôshiki*

jinzai kyōiku

人材教育

Training

Job training—*jinzai kyōiku*—is intended to improve the employee's skills so that they attain the required dexterity to execute their job. Training may be classroom-based, on the job, or perhaps via lectures. A new employee in a Japanese firm is not required to know anything, but will receive training and education in order to facilitate the performance of the task at hand. This idea of job training is carried out in Japanese companies with the assumption of life-time employment and simultaneous recruiting of new graduates, alongside the idea of seniority-based pay.

The training style in Japanese firms is heavily shaped by the assumption of life-time employment. Training is provided on the presumption that new recruits will avail themselves of the offered job security, and remain with the firm until retirement. Training a new employee with potential is viewed as an investment for the firm which increases the value of the employee. Japanese firms value new graduates who have potential, dividing them into "batches" that are provided with the same annual program of training.

Training can be formal, or merely through daily social contact with instructors, supervisors, or senior staff. This then connects with the idea of seniority-based pay, namely the assumption that since seniors are more knowledgeable due to long experience and long investment in training, they should receive higher status and more privileges. Seniority also determines promotion, benefits, and layoff alignment. Job rotation (*haichi tenkan*) is then used in order to disseminate the necessary skills through the firm. (E.O.)

See Also: *haichi tenkan, nenkō joretsu, shūshin kōyō*

jirei

辞令

Letter of appointment

The *jirei*, or letter of appointment, is a formal procedure which follows strict rules. *jirei* can be issued when there is a need to move employees within company branches or to hire new employees. Due to the practice of lifetime employment, *jirei* issued by senior members of a company carry significant weight.

A *saiyō jirei* (letter of employment) is issued to hire employees. These are formal papers containing the issuer's name, the recipient's name, and the date when they are to work. Employees in Japan do not enter a contract with their company—a contract being seen as unnecessary within a context of lifetime employment. One of the principal benefits of the use of *jirei* is order: in large companies, information may be distorted when passed on by word of mouth, whereas with *jirei* everything is formally written down. Moreover, for many Japanese companies, as well as their employees, the *jirei* still has important ceremonial significance.

Appointment through *jirei* leaves little room for the recipient to protest or negotiate. The position and the title of the employee can be adjusted without advance notice, and in some cases long-distance transfers may be effected without regard for a person's living arrangements.

However, the idea of order being imposed from the top down is decreasingly accepted by the younger generation. The economic recession, as well as the changing culture of the young, is forcing Japanese businesses to change, though the centrality of the belief in order means that this core is unlikely to completely disappear. With the restructuring of the Japanese business environment, *jirei* are losing the force they once had, but still remain an essential part of Japanese business culture. (N.O.)

See also: *kaisha, nenkō joretsu*

Just-in-time (JIT)

Lean Management

Just-in-time (JIT), also known as Lean Management, is a philosophy based on planned elimination of all waste, including inventory and associated carrying costs, thus to improve a business's return on investment. It was originally described as a strategy which aims at the production of the right amount of goods in the right place and at the right time to meet customer demand. The basic elements of JIT were adopted and developed by Toyota in the 1950s, and became famous as one of the most important components of the Toyota Production System. JIT applies primarily to repetitive manufacturing processes in which the same products and components are produced over and over again. The general idea is to establish flow processes by linking work centers so that there is an even, balanced flow of materials throughout the entire production process, similar to what is found in an assembly line. Implemented correctly, JIT can dramatically improve a manufacturing organization's quality, efficiency, and return on investment.

There are many key elements and benefits of JIT. First, it requires production leveling (*heijunka or 平準化*), so as to create a uniform load on all work centers by producing roughly the same mix of products each day, using a repeating sequence if several products are produced on the same line. Next is the reduction of setup times. Aiming for single digit setup times (less than 10 minutes) or "one touch" setup, through better planning, process redesign, and product redesign, allows the company to improve their bottom line, be more efficient, and focus on other areas that may need improvement. The reduction of lot sizes (manufacturing and purchase) is also necessary. Reducing setup times enables economical production of smaller lots, and necessitates close cooperation with suppliers. Delivery lead times can be reduced through close cooperation with suppliers, and possibly by inducing suppliers to relocate closer to the factory. Preventive maintenance is mandatory, and companies must use machine and worker idle time to maintain equipment and prevent breakdowns. Workers should be trained to operate several machines, and to perform maintenance tasks and quality inspections, in order to create a flexible work force. Employees who possess multiple skills can be used more efficiently and will allow companies to move and assign workers to where they are needed. Companies must also take into account supplier quality assurance; errors leading to defective items must be eliminated. (M.O.)

See also: *heijunka, jidōka, kaizen, kanban, keiretsu, muda-mura-muri*

jōshiki

常識

Common Sense

Common sense—*jōshiki*—is derived from language, knowledge, common practices, manners, and social structures, and is different for each culture. Even within a society, common sense changes over time, and different groups of people would have different *jōshiki* as shared by their members.

jōshiki is taken very seriously in Japan. With their emphasis on group harmony, the Japanese see *jōshiki* as the basic common ground that all members should share. Japanese people are very sensitive about having *jōshiki*.

jōshiki that relates to interaction with other people is considered especially important, being a critical element for communication and harmony. Use of language and manners are considered the most important but also the most difficult form of *jōshiki*. The use of *keigo* (敬語), language which shows respect and manners in conversation, is of absolute importance in business and formal situations, and is expected of all adults. However, the use and teaching of *keigo* has declined in recent years, and many people are especially confused by the differences between *kenjōgo* (謙譲語) and *sonkeigo* (尊敬語), the language used for top-down communication and vice versa. Misuse of *keigo* could damage the speaker's status as having *jōshiki* (常識). People thus buy books or attend sessions to ensure that they are using the correct *keigo*, and magazines may run such things as "lists of *keigo* often used incorrectly" or "incorrect *keigo* used by young people."

Manners are another important *jōshiki*. Manners in daily life are considered basic *jōshiki*, yet there are special manners for special ceremonial occasions, such as weddings, funerals, and ancestral worship. Rituals have special procedures that are complicated and difficult to learn. Bookstores have special sections on them.

Japanese learn *jōshiki* from a young age, both from family and by being in a group. Parents make great efforts to ensure that their children have enough *jōshiki*, and to a person who lacks it people often say *oya no kao ga mitemitai*, meaning that they would like to see the reaction of the parent who has brought up such a child. Time for learning *jōshiki* is given in school, and people are expected to have acquired sufficient *jōshiki* by the time they go out to work. The older one is, the more serious a matter this becomes, and no allowances are made for lack of *jōshiki* after entering a company. Job-hunting university students in Japan may take multiple examinations, including an exam to test *jōshiki* called the *ippan jōshiki* test. This includes tests on literature, mathematics, politics, sciences, English, and current events. Because the exam concerns current news and events, study books for the examination are updated every year. Moreover, *jōshiki* is tested in the interview: the interviewer does not only note the content of the conversation, but also the manner, appearance, and use of language as signs of appropriate *jōshiki*. Because of its importance, there are special schools—not cheap—for learning *jōshiki* for job hunting as well as free sessions in universities and large job fairs, and extensive literature in bookstores.

See also: *keigo (sonkeigo, kenjōgo, teineigo)*, *tateshakai*, *shushoku katsudō*

kabushiki mochiai

株式持合い

Cross-shareholding

kabushiki mochiai is a method in which firms agree to purchase significant amounts of each others' stocks. The West knows this as cross-shareholding. This strategy is adopted between banks and companies, as well as customers and their suppliers—it is not just company to company. This provides mutual benefits at moments when they are most needed but can sometimes also be harmful. Cross shareholding is not unique to Japan but is prominent there because of Japan's group-based business culture.

The practice started with the *zaibatsu* (財閥) holding groups around the end of World War II. In the beginning, companies used this method to form solid and reliable bases of stockholders to promote company growth. This worked well. During the crisis in the early 60s, banks bought stocks to promote a quick recovery of the stock market. Once the stock market started to show signs of a recovery, the banks sold the shares to individuals, while monitoring who bought them to prevent one individual or group from gaining too much shareholder power.

Cross-shareholding is not as common in other countries, where takeovers are preferred to mutual stock sharing. This reflects the Western mindset: Japanese companies place a great deal of importance on having good relationships and being in a group, while outside Japan companies tend to undermine the power of groups and place less emphasis on long-term relations.

Cross-shareholding is not only used to benefit the present financial standing of the company, but also to develop relationships between groups of companies and encourage future business. Funds invested can be used to ensure that goods will be both produced and consumed, bringing a steady income to the company and helping provide for overall growth. Cross-shareholding also prevents takeovers, and so allows corporate managers the safe space they need in which to engage in new projects while also thinking of the long-term health of the company. Additionally, cross-shareholding promotes stability in times of economic crisis, since companies can rely on their stable investors to purchase stock whenever needed—although this security can break down during periods of severe crisis.

This system blocks the entrance of foreign companies into the Japanese market. Companies engaged in cross-shareholding are likely to deal exclusively with each other and not with foreign businesses. This exclusiveness may generate security, but it also tends to harm Japanese companies globally, and may be unhelpful during times of economic adversity, while investors could be opposed to putting money into a system that is unwelcoming to foreign companies.

Recently, companies involved in long-term cross-shareholding have been suffering from stock depreciation. Cross-shareholding may in part be to blame, since investors may perceive signs of danger in the investment behavior of the partners—if company A raises its shares in its cross-shareholder partner B, other shareholders may see this as a sign that something is wrong with company B and so divest. (R.C.)

See Also: *kabushiki kaisha, kaisha, shudan shugi*

kaigi

会議

Business Meeting

The Japanese *kaigi*—"meeting" or "conference," whether in a business or a family setting—truly reflects the Japanese culture of group orientation, in which open conflicts are taboo and members should strive for a feeling of one-ness. They are strict about the way of doing things (*shikata* or 仕方), and value harmony (*wa*). Japanese people could be described as citizens of group orientation (*shudan shugi*), and because of this it usually takes longer making decisions in Japan.

kaigi is very strict in applying traditional rules of seating arrangements. The *kamiza* (上座) is the side that is the farthest away from the incoming door, where the higher-ranked person sits; this is usually a wall with a grand painting or respectful pictures of previous CEOs. Lower-ranked individuals sit at the *shimoza* (下座), closest to the door and opposite the *kamiza*. The traditional Japanese seating is also reflected in daily occurrences such as dinner, drinking events, and *kaigi* between two different companies. Japanese people are expected to know the seating arrangements as a form of good manners.

kaigi are very slow, since the Japanese do not come to a conclusion unless everyone has presented a viewpoint and supports the final solution. Japanese culture does not tolerate the majority rule, but tries to include everyone's ideas and come to a consensus in which everyone is happy and respected. From a Western perspective this can be annoying; for the Japanese it respects group orientation and preserves the *wa*.

nemawashi (根回し), prior consultation, may take place before a *kaigi*. Executives may be asked for suggestions and opinions before the meeting and proposals modified in advance, so avoiding open conflicts. As a result, the proposals will contain everyone's suggestions, which is ultimately the sign that the participants have been respected.

kazoku kaigi (家族会議) means family meeting. *nemawashi* is not necessarily practiced before such an event, since conflicts are not considered taboo among family members. Although *kazoku kaigi* is not adopted in all family households, it is used when a family gets together to discuss rules or vacations. It is often pictured as being held at a dinner table or in the living room, where every family member is able to physically participate. Depending on the situation, a family would come to a mutual agreement, or the father—who often holds the superior position—would make the final call after everyone's input. (Y.S.)

See also: *nemawashi, shudan shugi*

kaisha

会社

Company

A *kaisha* (company, corporation, firm) is a legal entity or corporate body, privately or publicly owned, which performs the role of linking product, sector, and capital markets. There are crucial differences between Japanese *kaisha* as compared to most companies in the world, specifically in regard to human resource management, firm mentality, production management, and strategies.

Human resource management in a *kaisha* is mainly based on seniority-based salary and life-time employment. These features bind employees strongly to their employers, and Japanese companies are often thought of as a second family. Indeed, the level of involvement a Japanese worker has with his company is comparable to that of a family.

A Japanese employee (*salaryman* or サラリマン) will likely work for one company for his or her entire working life. In a typical career, a person enters a company right after graduating from university and successfully passing a strict and complex application process. New employees will start with low-level work and a low salary, but as they advance up the corporate ladder their responsibilities and salary will increase. They do not have to know about the specific work-related procedures before they start, as these will be taught through repetition and oversight from their *senpai* (employees who have worked longer at the company). Employees will likely get insight into all sections of the company and will have to perform all kinds of work for at least a short period of time.

The *salaryman*'s work will most likely be time-consuming, and he will spend time with his boss and colleagues at after-work *nomikai* (drinking sessions) where they talk about private issues as well as business, sometimes even conducting business deals with trade partners in a relaxed environment. He will hesitate to ask for a day off unless he is sick or one of his relatives has passed away. He will not lightly decide to change jobs, because after spending years in one company and working his way up to a good salary, he will be reluctant to have to undergo the process once again from the lowest level. In return for his dedicated service, he will get benefits from his company such as bonuses, health care, status, and social security as well as the very high possibility of life-time employment.

Due to economic crises and future uncertainty, Japanese companies are starting to change their management techniques and strategies. An increasing number are rethinking the concept of life-time employment and seniority-based pay. Hiring part-time workers or introducing performance-based remuneration makes it easier to react to a crisis. A full-time worker cannot easily be fired, and during times of major crisis the company performs less flexibly. One consequence of abandoning the life-time employment policy is the loss of the trust employees feel toward their employers. Without the guarantee of life-time employment, an employee's feeling of dedication will decrease. In the near future, the Japanese *kaisha* will have to decide whether to continue with traditional Japanese methods or instead to adopt alternative human resource concepts. In the interim, they risk the worst of both worlds. (L.S.)

See also: *nenkyō joretsu, salaryman, senpai, keiretsu*

kaizen

改善

Kaizen

kaizen is the Japanese term for "Continuous Improvement" It is the most important and best-known concept in Japanese management and in fact the key to Japan's competitive success. The *kanji* 改善 is comprised of change (改) and good (善). *kaizen* does not only mean continuous improvement in a corporate setting but also in personal life, home life, social life, and working life. When applied to company and management processes, *kaizen* refers to continuously improving them, a credo for all -managers and workers alike. The *kaizen* philosophy suggests that human beings should make constant improvement efforts. *kaizen* is a gradual, unending improvement, doing little things better, setting and achieving ever higher standards.

kaizen is therefore a broader concept, which covers some Japanese management techniques including total quality management (TQM), just-in-time (JIT), total productive maintenance (TPM), policy deployment, and *jidoka*. Total quality Management (TQM) is an integrated management philosophy and set of practices that emphasizes management performance and quality, and involves everybody in the company. *Just-in-Time* is one of the key components of the Toyota Production System (TPS), which is to produce the necessary parts in the necessary quantities at the necessary time. TPM (or Total Productivity Maintenance) is a maintenance system which involves a newly defined concept for maintaining plants and equipment. It focuses on improving equipment quality and seeks to maximize equipment efficiency through a total system of preventive maintenance. Policy deployment or *hoshinkanri* is a process of achieving corporate objectives by establishing policies, targets and priorities. Management sets clear targets to guide everyone and provides leadership for all *kaizen* activities directed toward achieving the targets. In addition to Just-in-Time system, many Japanese companies employ *jidōka,* an autonomation system.

The best-known segment of the *kaizen* is management-oriented *kaizen*. It deals with the critical strategic issues to keep up progress and morale. Problem-solving expertise as well as professional and engineering knowledge are among the requirements. The seven basic tools of quality are used for analytical problem-solving: cause-and-effect diagram (also known as the "fishbone" or Ishikawa diagram), check sheet, control charts, histogram, Pareto chart, scatter diagram, and stratification (or, flow chart).

Group oriented *kaizen* involves quality control (QC) circles and small-group activities. Team members in the QC circles identify problems and their causes, analyze the causes, implement and test countermeasures, and establish new standards and procedures. Small-group activities strengthen teamwork, help members share and coordinate their roles, improve communication between workers, improve morale, help workers develop new skills, knowledge, and cooperative attitudes, and improve labor management relations.

Individual oriented *kaizen* focuses on *suggestion systems* and the idea that employees should work smarter, not necessarily harder. The individual provides suggestions on how to improve a work area. The key to success is to provide employees with the education needed for quality suggestions. Employees need problem-solving skills to make their jobs easier, safer, more productive, and less time and cost consuming.

See also: *jidōka,* Just-in-time (JIT), *kanban*

kanban

看板

Card

A *kanban* system uses cards, or *kanban*, to track parts during manufacturing processes. *kanban* contain information on the identity, origin, destination, and quantity of the parts. The usage of *kanban* became part of the Toyota Production System developed by former Vice President Taiichi Ohno in the 1950s, which employed a Just-In-Time inventory system.

The *kanban* system is a form of "pull" system. In a pull system, additional parts or materials are requested as needed. In contrast, a push system often employs a complex Material Requirements Planning (MRP) schedule, where computer software is used to predict the need for each part. Parts are produced or delivered independently of need, following only the MRP schedule. Pull systems tend to have a lower inventory of parts as well as more frequent deliveries. As a result, pull systems like the *kanban* system are used primarily in Just-In-Time production, keeping inventories low and minimizing storage costs.

The Toyota Dual-*kanban* system uses bins to hold a small number of parts—no more than 1/10 of the daily requirement. In the factory, there are workers who produce parts and workers that use the parts to produce the product. Production workers manufacture parts to fill empty bins marked with a Production-*kanban*, producing the exact number of parts specified on the Production-*kanban*. The Production-*kanban* is then replaced with a Conveyance-*kanban*, and the bin is sent to the workers who use the parts in production. When the bin of parts arrives, the Conveyance-*kanban* is removed and sent back to the part's production workers. The production workers replace the Conveyance-*kanban* with a Production-*kanban* and produce more parts as needed. The Conveyance-*kanban* is often placed on empty bins when being sent back to the part's production workers, so that bins for parts can be reused. Therefore, at any given point in time, there are only a few filled bins of parts, as opposed to large storage bins for parts in warehouses. Despite the low inventory, parts will still always be available for the workers using them.

Under the *kanban* system, no parts are produced until a Production-*kanban* requests them, and parts are produced exactly as the Production-*kanban* specifies. Furthermore, only the exact number of parts requested is produced, even if production workers are idle between requests. To control inventory, managers determine how many *kanban* of each type are in use in the factory at any given time. Managing the number of *kanban* in the factory controls inventory because empty bins without a *kanban* attached are ignored. In this way, managers can control the speed of production, and adjust very quickly to changes in demand and work environment.

Using procedures such as the *kanban* system, Just-In-Time production can be more efficient and cost-effective than Material Requirements Planning schedules. MRP requires managers to predict demand for parts and products and create a production schedule accordingly. Just-In-Time production with *kanban* does not rely on predicting future demand because managers can quickly and easily adjust the number of parts and products being produced by changing the *kanban*.

Since its introduction, the *kanban* system has been updated to make use of technology. Electronic *kanban* are now used, and a large amount of research and analysis has been done to determine the number of *kanban* and bins needed to optimize the efficiency of the factory with a minimum inventory of parts. In addition, some companies with simpler manufacturing processes have combined the Material Requirements Planning push system with a Just-In-Time single-*kanban* pull system. (J.S.)

See also: *jidōka,* Just-in-time (JIT)

kanji

漢字

Chinese characters

kanji is the name given to the aspect of the Japanese logographic script that is imported from the Chinese writing system. In Japanese there are four main writing systems; *kanji*, which are the Chinese characters; *hiragana* and *katakana*, referred to as *kana* and essentially script based; and occasional Latin letters known as *romaji*. In Japanese the majority of native words contain *kanji*, but the use of *kanji* is mostly limited to nouns, adjectives, and verb stems. In most cases, *hiragana* is used for verb conjugation and linking of adjectives. This is therefore different from the Chinese system, where only the *kanji* characters are used. *kanji* is used extensively in the workplace, and a grasp of it is absolutely vital: professional communications are all written with large amounts of *kanji* so as to appear more formal, even if the *kanji* is not one that is commonly in use.

kanji seems to have been imported to Japan from China via the goods trade around 2,000 years ago. At the time Japan had no writing system of its own, and so the *kanji* brought over by Chinese immigrants steadily took hold.

As time passed, both *hiragana* and *katakana* were developed, since the Japanese language differed in spoken form from Chinese. This difference meant that *kanji* characters with a definite meaning in Chinese would be used in Japanese purely for the sound that they offered, rendering the written form somewhat confusing. In order to overcome this, the systems of *hiragana* and *katakana* were developed in parallel to give a sound to a very simple character and remove any confusion used in using a *kanji* out of context. But even with the introduction of *hiragana* and *katakana*, the reading of *kanji* remains fiendishly difficult as each *kanji* can have ten or more different readings, depending on the context or various other factors.

Generally speaking, *kanji* can be split into *onyomi* (音読み) and *kunyomi* (訓読み) readings, where *onyomi* represents the Chinese reading of a character, and *kunyomi* represents the Japanese reading. *onyomi* is used in the majority of multi-*kanji* compound words which represent the same idea or meaning in both Chinese and Japanese, and is read in a similar way in Japanese as it would be in Chinese, save for a few differences to adapt the sound for Japanese pronunciation. On the other hand, *kunyomi* is used for words where the Japanese have adopted a *kanji* from Chinese, but adapted the reading of it to what already existed in the spoken language. This means that most *kanji* in Japanese have many different readings and it can be difficult to know at first glance exactly how to read them in a sentence.

Although there are estimated to be in excess of 50-100,000 *kanji*, proficiency sufficient for reading literature, business transactions, and newspapers requires mastery only of the so-called *jōyō kanji* (常用漢字), comprising 1,945 characters. In Japanese schools this is expected to be achieved by ninth grade. The highest-level examination for *kanji* in Japan is the Kanji Kentei test which tests around 6,000 characters.

kanji is seen as the most professional way of writing communications, and while *kanji* compounds are often written in *hiragana* in day-to-day use, the corresponding *kanji* would be used in formal communication. The level of *kanji* used in such correspondence is often of a higher level than the one taught in the schools, so high proficiency in *kanji* is strongly desired by Japanese companies. (Jo.S.)

See also: *hiragana, katakana, keigo, meishi, tateshakai*

karaoke

カラオケ

Karaoke

Karaoke is a popular form of entertainment that was invented by Daisuke Inoue in Kobe. It is an interactive game in which one sings along to a musical backing track. These sing-along machines first became popular in Japan in the 1970s and soon spread to the rest of Asia and America. *Karaoke* has now become Japan's fourth most popular form of entertainment, behind cinema, restaurants, and bars. *Karaoke* consists of the words *Kara*, derived from *karappo* meaning "empty," and *oke*, shortened from *okesutura* meaning "orchestra."

The early *karaoke* machine comprised a microphone and a coin box attached to a tape recorder. Inoue would lend out the device along with cassette tapes with instrumental versions of songs. One would sing along to the tape while reading the lyrics off a piece of paper; nowadays big TV screens show the lyrics as well as mood-enhancing images.

Perhaps because Japanese houses are built very close together, the *karaoke* box was developed. These were originally old freight cars, adapted to act as soundproof rooms in which singers could sing as loud as they wanted without embarrassment. These boxes could be rented by the hour, and catered to a younger market which lacks the money for hostesses in bars. Over the years the boxes have appeared everywhere, in both rural and urban areas. The number of *karaoke* boxes peaked at 160,680 in 1996, compared to 52,578 in 1990, and 131,200 in 2006.

In the 1990s *karaoke* spread to the rest of Asia and then to the United States, Canada, Australia, and other Western countries. *Karaoke* machines were sold not strictly for the purpose of *karaoke* singing, but as home theater systems to enhance the quality of television watching. In Asia, meanwhile, people within the industry saw the potential in *karaoke* and started to use it as lounge and nightclub entertainment. In Japan, about 80% of the 350,000 bars in the country have *karaoke* machines and about four-fifths of adults say they have performed *karaoke*.

karaoke became popular for a number of reasons. One of the most important reasons for its popularity is that it is a way to communicate with each other. In particular, it is a way for people to express themselves by avoiding direct face-to-face communication. It is a place where the hierarchy between colleagues can be broken down and office tension can be released. The image of *salarymen* in a *karaoke* bar after work has been portrayed many times in books, movies, and *manga*. The *karaoke* can be compared to the role that *geisha*s played during parties. They would draw people together, encourage clients to sing, and help them communicate.

A recent development is the *hitokara*, which is short for *hitori* (single) *karaoke*. People would go alone to the *hitokara*, perhaps to practice their singing before they sing in front of friends and colleagues, or just for the love of music. (S.A.)

See also: *awase, ishin denshin, kaigi, marugakae, nomikai/bonenkai*

karōshi

過労死

Death through overwork

karōshi means "death through overwork." The two main causes of *karōshi* deaths are heart attack or stroke, due to stress and fatigue from long hours in the office. Alongside these, there are many cases of work stress leading to personal problems and in turn to suicide. Japan has faced these tragedies for a long time but is still in search of a way to prevent them.

Japan's rapid growth in the post–World War II era is regarded as the trigger for *karōshi*. In this era, known as the "Japanese post-war economic miracle," each citizen's hard work was richly rewarded, but led as a byproduct to *karōshi*. The first known case of such death occurred in 1969, when a 29-year-old who worked in the shipping department of a big newspaper company died from a stroke after working for forty consecutive days. However, it was not until the middle of 1980s—and after several moderately high-ranked and otherwise healthy employees died from it—that special attention began to be paid.

The cause seems simply to be the Japanese employees' loyalty and willingness to work hard. Statistics show that each Japanese worker averages about two hours' overtime a day, total of about 10 per week. Working late at night, in some cases all night, and during holidays, thus leads to illness and death. And before the health problems, personal problems arise: addicted to work in the office, employees tend to forget about family members, falling out of touch with them despite ostensibly living together under one roof. Some employees are more loyal to the company they work for than to their own families.

The peak of deaths came during the 1990s, after the collapse of the bubble economy forced companies to cut down on the number of employees, but not on the amount of overall work, forcing each employee to work harder. According to Labor Ministry statistics, when *karōshi* was declared as a term in 1987, twenty-one cases occurred that year, thirty cases in 1989, but over a thousand people died each year in the 1990s, excluding suicides. Work-related stress is common in every country, but at nothing like the levels seen in Japan. It is not unusual to see workers work overtime till very late at night; and in many cases overtime is unpaid.

The Japanese authorities have introduced measures to decrease the number of deaths by overwork. In 2016, 107 karōshi cases, including 84 suicides and suicide attempts were reported. Measures include interval times, an increase in public holidays, compulsory stress tests for employees in large companies and the placing of legal limits on overtime work. (A.T.)

See also: *ganbaru*

keigo

敬語

Polite Speech

keigo broadly refers to the honorific way of speaking in the Japanese language. It can be directly translated into English as "Respectful Language." *keigo* is one of the defining and enduring characteristics of Japanese, and can be broken down into three separate categories: *sonkeigo* (尊敬語), respectful or honorific language; *kenjōgo* (謙譲語), humble language; and *teineigo*, polite language. The term "honorific" therefore describes both *keigo* as a whole, and also the subcategory *sonkeigo*, though they have different meanings. Essentially, *keigo* refers to the distinctive style of speech or writing used to show respect to persons, and sometimes to sacred things such as shrines or temples. In this sense, it symbolizes the hierarchical disparity or similarity between participants in a conversation. This is consistent with Japanese society itself, in which hierarchical relationships are important—within a company, for example—and through concepts such as the *senpai–kōhai* relationship.

The term *keigo* was invented by scholars of the Meiji era (1868-1912) to describe something that had presumably always existed and was omnipresent but had yet to be discretely defined. *keigo* is based around the observance of the difference in status between the speaker and the addressee. The Japanese concept of status differs from that of other cultures. In Western cultures, the category of "equals" is very broad; in Japan the slightest difference may result in an elevated status, and in fact people treat somebody of the same status as having a higher status. The factors that determine status include rank and position, social status, age, and gender. Because *keigo* is such an ingrained part of Japanese society, failure to employ it accurately can be considered extremely offensive—even if you are a foreigner, as it is assumed that you understand such concepts if you can speak the language

The first subcategory of *keigo*, *sonkeigo*, can be described as respectful or honorific language. It is used when talking about or to an addressee to whom respect must be accorded; it cannot be used to talk about oneself. *sonkeigo* is usually directed towards people in a relatively higher position of power, for example superiors at work or customers in a store. *sonkeigo* may be achieved by substituting a normal word for its counterpart in *sonkeigo*, or by transforming it using a set of rules.

kenjogo, or humble language, is utilized when the speaker is describing to someone from the out-group the actions of themselves or people in their in-group, in a humbling manner. There is a subtle implication that one's actions are undertaken in order to assist the person from the outside group. This is distinct from *sonkeigo*, in which the addressee is exalted rather than the speaker humbled. The in-group/out-group principle is critical in Japanese culture. Members of someone's in-group include people within the same family, circle, club, or place of employment. People in an out-group obviously comprise people outside these groups and include foreigners. As with *sonkeigo*, *kenjogo* replaces certain standard words with particular *kenjogo* words, and words may also be adapted according to particular rules.

teineigo, or polite language, is less complex and demanding than the previous two subcategories. It is the first form of Japanese taught to new learners of the language and is used when the speaker wants to be polite without needing to observe hierarchical differences.

keigo is necessary in a number of different situations. At universities a strict hierarchy must be observed, both between students and teachers, but also between students themselves based on seniority and responsibility within clubs and circles. For loosely structured or non-structured settings such as neighborhood groups or social clubs, the hierarchy is less formal and generally polite language is used. Polite speech is generally also used for first meetings when there is no clear disparity in rank apparent due to age, occupation, or social status. Where there is a clear difference, *sonkeigo* and/or *kenjogo* may be used, depending on the speakers. Participants in a long-term relationship of any type are still expected to observe the hierarchical difference; the duration of a relationship does not change the relationship into one in which both parties are equal. Therefore, once the relationship is established, whichever type of *keigo* is used initially is likely to be used for the entire length of the relationship, even if the person who was initially ranked lower goes on to achieve a higher status.

Finally, one of the most salient implementations of *keigo* is in the workplace. Length of service tends to be more important than age. Therefore, someone who has been at a company for longer than another person will be treated as a *senpai* (more experienced person) or *meue* (目上 or senior), by the less experienced *kōhai* or *meshita* (目下 or junior). Where there are factors that cross—for example where by one measure one person is higher, but by another measure the other person is higher—rank and position are the most influential factors in determining hierarchy. In this way, it is not uncommon for a manager to be younger than his or her subordinates, yet still be able to speak down to them. Because the Japanese workplace follows strict rules and traditions, observance of *keigo* is a necessity. (M.T.)

See also: *daigaku, senpai - kōhai, nengajō – shochûmimmai*

keiretsu

系列

Conglomerate

keiretsu is the term for a conglomerate or financial group. Traditionally, *keiretsu* are vertically organized, consisting of many small and medium-sized businesses that all come together to form one unified company, such as Toyota. They are the descendents of the *zaibatsu* which once controlled most of Japanese industry. After their dissolution, the *zaibatsu* rebuilt themselves in the early 1950s as *keiretsu*, focusing on large industries, mainly concerned with automotives or electronics, examples being Toyota, Honda, Sony, and Toshiba. These *keiretsu* were very similar to *zaibatsu* (財閥), except that they eliminated the *zaibatsu* families which had controlled them in the past.

The firms are often centered around a large bank, and the defining features of *keiretsu*, which have indeed become emblematic of Japanese industry itself, are lifetime employment, seniority-based pay, trade unions, and consensual capitalism. Cross-shareholding (*kabushiki mochiai*) has been developed by the larger parent companies of the *keiretsu* in order to protect the infant businesses allied with them from foreign companies. Companies within a single *keiretsu* hold stock in each other to cement their bonds. This process allows the *keiretsu* to ensure their stability and so focus on long-term growth; since they have tied their fates together, when stocks for one company in the group grow, they will all grow, and when losses are incurred, they can be split over all the members.

The subcontracting system characteristic of the *keiretsu* was also very important in establishing their importance. Because these groups were made up of many firms, some similar and some widely different from the others in the group, *keiretsu* no longer had to outsource but could subcontract their work to another smaller company within the *keiretsu*. Because they were subcontracting their work within the *keiretsu*, the larger companies could push more capital through the smaller firms in order to get more out of them. This created a system in which both the smaller firms and the large parent firms were dependent on each other for success.

Three other features are traditional characteristic of the *keiretsu*. The first is the predominance of exports over imports, which is a result of the lack of competition within companies in Japan. Second is a predominance of employment over productivity, stemming from the management practice of seniority-based pay and lifetime employment. Third is the preference for market share over corporate profit. Given the loss-making strategy within business abroad—that is, *keiretsu* sell in mass quantities at low prices—as well as the massive fixed costs of creating and maintaining these firms, they are forced to concentrate on market share. This fixed cost has also led people to believe that another goal of the *keiretsu* is to block market entry to foreign firms, or even upcoming domestic firms. Given the dominance of the *keiretsu*, it is very difficult for a start-up company or a company that does not already have a foothold in the Japanese market to challenge them.

While all these factors are still widely true of *keiretsu* today, recent years have seen new directions of evolution. Rather than the vertically structured entities of the past, *keiretsu* have become horizontally structured in order to compensate for the weaker economy: rather than focusing on the success of the parent company, companies instead support each other and so create one strong entity. This horizontal structure reduces risk for other companies involved, as well as for transaction partners and investors. Additionally, since the economic bubble burst in Japan, banks have taken less of a central role in *keiretsu*, with financial support coming from other sources, such as foreign investment and non-bank investment. The clearest example of the new form of *keiretsu* is 7&i Holdings. This corporation is a financial group that spans several varied markets including grocery stores, convenience stores, financial services, department stores, and information technology services. This group is able to support itself financially, support its employees with the 7&i life design branch, and has several committees to manage every aspect of the group, as well as a CEO and a shareholder's meeting. (S.T.)

See also: *zaibatsu, kigyō kumiai, shūshin koyō, kabushiki mochiai*

keiyaku

契約

Contract

A contract is a voluntary agreement between two parties, which can be enforced legally, under which both parties are responsible for fulfilling the duties agreed. Good business relationships have been a major factor in Japan's economic success, and this is especially evident in negotiations over contracts. The main purpose of businesses is generally said to be to make profit; however, that is not the main value in Japanese enterprises, and there are vast differences between the Japanese business culture and their Western counterparts as regards contractual negotiations. When negotiating a contract with Japanese firms, it is important to have an understanding of the way business is done in Japan. Contracts may serve as doors to establishing long-term commitments.

Contracts are an important part of Japanese management, because while contract negotiations are taking place the Japanese are long-term-commitment-minded. Japanese firms send company employees to establish long-lasting relationships with the consumer and make sure they are comfortable with the terms of the contract. Harmony has always been a significant aspect of Japanese business culture, and is valued greatly when building good relationships with the consumer. In these contract negotiations, the company employee conducts business with the customer on a personal and emotional level. It is common for an employee from a Japanese firm to engage in small talk with a business partner or a client before discussing business. By doing so, the business partner or customer will reveal more information on their likes and dislikes, which is of great importance when it comes to understanding consumer behavior and satisfaction. The Japanese spend more time up front with a potential customer or supplier before making a commitment.

Western firms would focus on finalizing all terms of the agreement as soon as possible in order to be efficient with time. The Japanese are more flexible as regards changing certain contractual agreements. Flexibility on the part of the Japanese can be seen as a way of looking after business partners or customers even after a contract has been finalized. However, this can also be perceived as indecisiveness, which could lead to conflict with foreign business partners who are more accustomed to keeping the terms of the contract strictly unchanged.

When establishing the terms, duties, and responsibilities of a contract in Japan, one must bear in mind that Japanese people communicate differently from Westerners. The Japanese tend to be vague and communicate implicitly; in consequence, there can be misunderstandings when contractual negotiations are taking place. To avoid conflict in business relationships, the terms of the contract must be communicated as clearly and explicitly as possible to the parties involved. Once the legal aspects of the contract have been established, the interests of both parties are protected by law; but recourse to the law is not common in Japan, due to the fact that the needs of the Japanese consumers are so well taken care of. (K.U.)

See also: *kaisha, shitauke*

kigyō kumiai

企業組合

Trade union

The *kigyō kumiai* (enterprise union) is considered a largely post-war phenomenon, consequent on the enactment of the Labor Union Law by the occupying powers. It is often cited as one of the three "pillars" of the Japanese management system and a source of competitive advantage which has contributed to the economic success of Japan in the 1970s. Today, enterprise unions account for more than 90% of all union and organized workers, and in contrast to the West where unions are mostly organized based on skills or job status, in Japan the union members of an enterprise union include all white-collar and blue-collar workers of a single company.

At the time of establishment under the Occupation authorities, the union structure was predominantly horizontal and union membership included 45% of all employees. The leadership of unions was extremely left-wing, often Communist, and fierce battle for control of the workplace lasted throughout the early 1950s. However, the departing of the Occupation authorities also saw the depoliticization of labor, a movement which is now considered by academics to have led to the development of enterprise unionism. The unionization rate was around one-third from 1955 to mid-1970s, and in spite of the establishment of the National Federation of Private Sector Unions in the late 1980s to co-ordinate union activities, the union rate has been on the decline since then and now stands at around 20%.

Although there are no legal restrictions which limit the number of unions allowed at a workplace, one union per enterprise is seen as the predominant mode. As a result, the main role of these enterprise unions has largely been based on the promotion of the company as a community which fosters workers' loyalty and identification.

The structure and relationship between the enterprise union and the company is often said to be another example of the Japanese "integrated social system." Firstly, Japanese enterprise unions do not exist as a separate entity from the company, and are often housed in the same building or location as the company. Secondly, a leading position in the enterprise union is often seen as an integral part of the training for efficient management. To avoid the obvious conflict of interest, employees are required to withdraw their membership of the union when they are promoted from the union to management positions. Interestingly, this unique interdependent relationship between the company and the enterprise union means that as a community, both entities are willing to cooperate in the common interest, their future prospects being seen to be essentially identical.

The advantage of the enterprise union system relies on the idea of mutual benefits. Both the company and the union are aware that for their best interest, they should limit the extent to which they stand against each other in bargaining. Since all the workers belong to the same union, it is not possible for management to set one group against another. However, if the union activities are too vigorous and disruptive, then damage may be caused which actually comes at the union members' own expense. As a result, vocal demonstrations are mostly held during lunch breaks or after working hours, and unless there is a total breakdown in trust, labor unrest and strikes are mostly avoided. In fact, these days, unions are often said to be even more committed to the long-term interest of the company than the management itself.

The decline in the unionization rate and in the role of the union can be explained by the numerous problems which had emerged by the end of the 1990s. On the whole, the voice of the unions in various issues is seen as weak and ineffectual. Data suggest that the effect of unions on salary and earnings are virtually non-existent due to improved laws governing working conditions. The increasing trend for Japanese companies to move into the service sectors also means that workers have become more skeptical about the ability of their unions to defend their jobs amid the waves of globalization. As the appeal of lifetime employment and seniority promotion start to wear thin for the young Japanese workers, talented employees are now less willing to base their careers on hard-to-sell company-specific skills. As a result, the role of enterprise unions has gradually been redirected to the development of more avenues for direct influence in the management. There seems to be a movement from collective bargaining to joint consultation where most issues are settled without confrontation. Furthermore, with new types of unions appearing, especially support groups for foreigners, it is expected that the identity issue which unions face will continue to cause cracks in the three pillars of the Japanese management system. (S.W.)

See also: *nenkō joretsu, shūshin joretsu, seishain*

kojin kigyō

個人企業

Private company/entrepreneurship

Japan is not usually perceived as a country of entrepreneurs. Rather, it is a country of lifetime employment and teamwork among employees who have a powerful unwritten allegiance to their company. The Japanese term for private company is *kojin kigyō*. However, from the mid-20th century and onwards, successful entrepreneurs have been notably absent in the Japanese market. Several theories have been proposed for this sudden lack of entrepreneurial success. It might have been "the homogeneity of the society, a non-confrontational mode of discussion and decision making, and a national sense of purpose" that attracted Japanese workers to a *kaisha* (corporation) rather than to entrepreneurship.

During the high-growth years in the latter half of the 20th century, many new companies were spawned through larger corporations spinning off new business activity as a new company within the group. That was seen as providing competitive advantage wherein resources and connections were retained within the corporate cultural circle.

But the years of high growth came to an end, and Japan was faced with a period of stagnant growth known as the "Lost Decade." Faced with this, some have begun to ask whether the powerful industrial system which had originally driven growth was not now, in these changed international conditions, actually a source of weakness.

Recently, the Japanese government has stepped up efforts to assist entrepreneurs through several government policies. New legal frameworks have been put in place, such as the venture capital investment law of 1998, and grants and incentive programs have been established to encourage entrepreneurialism in Japan.

Nevertheless, despite government assistance, Japan still has a significantly lower number of tech start-up companies than rival economies such as the United States and China. There are several reasons for this. For one thing, aspiring entrepreneurs face barriers in finding the three crucial components of success: finance, skilled employees, and customers. The Japanese cultural dream is still very much centered on studying hard at a school with a good reputation, so as to go to a high-ranked university, and thus find lifetime employment in a major company. It is also generally known that in Japanese firms, tacit knowledge (knowledge gained through experience) is favored over specialization. Similarly, incremental innovation is encouraged over radical innovation. Yet the biggest problem is arguably finding funding.

Although there are still many barriers that stand in the entrepreneur's way, these barriers are steadily weakening. With the help of government policies, as well as a change in the way Japanese society is run as a whole, entrepreneurship is gaining ground. (M.A.)

See also: *kaisha, shūshin koretsu*

konbini

コンビニ

Convenience Store

Konbini ("convenience store") were first implanted in Japan three decades ago, following the American model. Today a distinctly Japanese model has evolved and is sure to continue to evolve in line with consumer expectations. *konbini* have become a part of everyday life in Japan. They can be found on every street corner in major cities and are also present in small towns and rural areas. These are local shops open 24 hours a day, as well as on Sundays, which sell such everyday products as food, newspapers and magazines, and beverages. Alongside these staples, they may also purvey body care products, cosmetics, batteries, blank CDs, umbrellas, and comics.

It is said that the first convenience store opened in Dallas, Texas in 1927. The first one opened in Japan in 1969, and American-style Seven-Elevens began operations in 1974. Since then, large supermarkets and corporations have invested in the *konbini* industry. In 2018 there were more than 52,600 convenience stores with annual revenues totaling over 6.7 trillion yen.

Seven Eleven is Japan's top chain, closely followed by Lawson, Family Mart, and the now-merged Sunkus and Circle K. Lawson has opened a chain of "Natural Lawson" stores selling organic and health-orientated products and Lawson 100 selling all products for a 100 yen.

About 75% of the revenues of *konbini* come from food products, and half of these are fast food, side dishes, or fresh confectionaries, all delivered on a daily basis. Both fast-food restaurants and *konbini* sell ready-to-eat food, such as *bentō* (弁当) or *onigiri* (おにぎり or rice pressed into a ball the size of a fist)—the latter is popular in part because it is cheap.

Japanese *konbini* today offer a huge range of additional services. At most stores, customers can pay their utility bills—water, electricity, gas, telephone, etc.—through automated multi-purpose terminals. It is possible to pick up goods ordered over the Internet, buy tickets for concerts and movies, photocopy documents, and send faxes or charge their phones, while stocking up on bottled water, ice-cream, or imported wines. Another recent development is for stores to be fitted with ATMs, enabling them to fulfill many of the functions of a small bank.

One recent trend is for convenience stores to join up with companies in other sectors. More and more gas stations, video rental stores, and others are teaming up with *konbini* operators to add a convenience store to their outlets. These firms are keen to take advantage of the ability of 24-hour convenience stores to attract customers. (J.B.)

See also: *okyaku, bentō, arbaito - freeter - haken, depāto, daigaku*

kudōka

空洞化

Hollowing out

kudōka, translated as "hollowing out," refers to the dissolution of the manufacturing sector in Japan after the burst of the bubble economy in 1990. Because of lower input costs, many large manufacturing firms moved their operations overseas where they could develop a comparative advantage by being more efficient and thus more profitable. During the 1990s, domestic manufacturing employment in Japan fell from 15.9 million in 1990 to 13.2 million in 2000, while overseas manufacturing employment rose from 1.24 million to 2.81 million. As these numbers illustrate, the relocation of manufacturing activities overseas had drastic repercussions for the Japanese economy. Moreover, employment wasn't the only thing affected. An increase in foreign direct investment, which was needed to support the newly created entities overseas, also caused domestic output to fall and produced problems for smaller firms within the same industry.

A normal indication of a mature economy is a shift from the manufacturing industry to the service industry, and this natural deindustrialization is signaled by a decrease in manufacturing's share of total employment among other factors. In Japan, manufacturing's share of total employment fell from over 24% in 1994 to 20% in 2000. Nevertheless, this doesn't mean that the occurrence of *kudōka* in Japan is a typical case. After deindustrialization, when manufacturers produce more overseas and import domestically from their overseas ventures, positive signs of a strong economy both at home and abroad are to be expected. This is where Japan fell short. From 1991-2001, real GDP only averaged a 1.1% increase.

After World War II, Japanese manufacturers were lauded for catching up with the West, but after the burst of the bubble economy in 1990, it can be argued that this system has outgrown its effectiveness. Problems associated with the hollowing out of the Japanese economy are believed by many to be caused by the existing government structure in Japan, which can be said to be characterized by excessive administrative guidance and regulation of markets. With the addition of more manufacturing operations overseas, exports have become more competitive and have significantly expanded. At the same time, because of government-imposed barriers, imports have remained stagnant. Cheaper imports are blocked by tariffs in addition to inefficiencies caused by the distribution and retail systems in place. This has promoted the over-appreciation of the yen and the penalization of significant sectors of the domestic economy.

For small firms, in the 1990s, it was very hard to relocate operations overseas because they lacked the resources to make this possible. For them, *kudōka*, combined with the effects of the recession such as the inability of banks to extend long-term loans, was devastating. In the Ota ward of Tokyo, two-thirds of all small manufacturing firms were affected by larger companies shifting operations overseas. After firms relocated their operations and specifically their resources overseas, the links between assembler and supplier were severely strained. By 2001, the number of small-firm bankruptcies reached record highs. For these reasons, the effects of *kudōka* really hurt small Japanese manufacturing firms. (F.B.)

See also: *keiretsu, bunkatsu hoshiki*

kyūryō

給料

Salary

The *kyūryō* (salary) received by an employee in Japan comes in various forms. Most workers receive *kyūryō* in scheduled monthly payments. A Japanese salary is also partly paid in bonuses, which roughly accounts for more than 20% of a worker's annual earnings. Bonuses are paid out twice a year, in summer and winter. A company gauges an employee's work performance and distributes a bonus according to competence. In unionized companies collective bargaining would occur between representatives of employers and trade unions to set the amount of bonus distributed in total. A company's economic performance for the year is therefore critical at these collective bargaining sessions in deciding upon the amount of money allocated towards bonuses. This further motivates workers to do their best.

Non-scheduled payments can be accrued by working overtime, something which is generally encouraged in Japanese companies. Lifetime employment also creates *kyūryō* in the form of various allowances: employees receive allowances for taking up new job positions, or cost-of-living allowances for moving to a new location. Since employees will be with the company for their entire working lives, companies will also offer allowances for education in order to learn a new skill and bolster their value to the company. An employee can even be rewarded for having a perfect attendance or good performance.

After Japan's participation in World War II, three fundamental ideologies arose that were implemented into Japanese business practices: lifetime employment, *nenkō-joretsu* (the seniority system), and enterprise unionism. These three ideologies were partly the cause of Japan's rapid economic growth after the war, and it was thus that the different forms of *kyūryō* took shape. Japanese firms utilized the *nenkō-joretsu* (seniority system or 年功序列) as the basis to determine and distribute the *kyūryō* evenly and fairly amongst its employees. The seniority-based pay system worked by increasing a worker's *kyūryō* according to their age and the years of service employed in the company. The seniority-based salaries meant that every worker would receive a higher income the longer they worked at the firm, irrespective of performance. Young workers would enter the company with different abilities but start off with the same *kyūryō*. This created a work environment that was tuned more towards being supportive of one another and gave less reason for employees to feel like they were in constant competition.

After the burst of the "bubble economy" in the latter half of the 1990s, Japan fell into financial crisis. Realizing that the seniority-based pay system would not help Japan into recovery, Japanese firms sought other practices of *kyūryō* distribution. Firms began to adopt the *seikashugi* (performance-based pay system or 成果主義). Under this new system, the length of time an employee had served under a company no longer played a part in determining *kyūryō*. Employees were now paid on the basis of productivity and performance. However, this form of distributing salaries was not without negative side effects. With the seniority system it is far easier to allocate resources around the company during times of recession, as the *kyūryō* paid out is very flexible. The gap between employees' salaries is not as distinctive and thus creates motivation for employees to work hard. With the *seikashugi* pay system an employee's *kyūryō* increases based on their performance, which makes it much harder for companies to guarantee lifetime employment and ensure the safety of employees' jobs during a recession. When companies start handing out *kyūryō* based on individual performance, a distinctive gap between employees' *kyūryō*s appears. These factors reduce employees' motivation, as they are plagued by thoughts of job insecurity and feel a destructive sense of competition with their co-workers. (A.C.)

See also: *kigyō kumiai, nenkō joretsu, shūshin koyō*

māketingu

マーケティング

Marketing

Marketing is an integrated process through which companies create value for consumers, and forge strong relationships so as to capture that consumer base and derive future value from it. Historically, Japanese companies have been intensely committed to *māketingu* (marketing), spending millions of dollars on it every year.

After World War II, Japan's main focus was on creating sufficient supplies to satisfy consumer needs, and it began to adapt technology from developed countries focused on improving the quality of its products. Despite the recession in the 1990s, Japan has maintained its position as the world's second largest economy, with a GDP equal to about two-thirds that of the United States. Although Japan is dependent on imports of raw materials, it remains a world leader in the manufacture of cars, ships, robots, and machines, and is also one of the biggest donors of Official Development Assistance. A distinctive marketing strategy lies behind Japan's economic development.

The major characteristic of Japanese marketing is its customer focus: the consumers' wants are the drivers of all strategic marketing decisions, and companies undertake extensive market research to determine what these wants are. The corporate marketing approach is communications and human-relations oriented, and emphasis is placed on building strong and long-term relationships based on trust.

The emergence of different consumer groups in the post-crisis era has had a great impact on Japanese companies' marketing activities. For example, the group comprised of single working women has become a key consumer group over the past few decades. Since most of these women earn money from working and often still live with their parents, they have a considerable income to spend on travel, fashion, brand goods, and beauty. Japanese companies thus often provide special products targeting them. Another new consumer group is aged retirees who have accumulated their income and received *taishokukin*, the retirement benefits for workers. Because they have both money and time, they tend to be an active consumer group and thus are also the subject of great interest by Japanese companies.

New marketing channels such as cyber marketing and mobile marketing are being developed in order to grasp consumer trends more quickly and precisely. Transformation of consumer behavior and advances in technology has created multi-channel marketing, including Internet-based promotion which attracts potential customers by adverts on websites, banners, emails, etc., and a rapidly growing emphasis on mobile marketing.

Brand orientation has been another distinctive feature of Japanese marketing in recent decades. Japanese consumers tended to consider the brand as a guarantee of quality, with well-known global brands and traditional Japanese companies thereby becoming highly competitive. Since the image of the brand has a significant impact on the company's business opportunities, Japanese companies have employed a brand-driven customer relationship program in order to maintain a good brand image which fits customer demand. However, the situation is changing little by little. Brand loyalty is decreasing and the corporate brand image is becoming more and more ineffective. As consumers are no longer willing to blindly follow corporate brand image in making purchasing decisions, Japanese companies are switching to product brands rather than corporate brands, through such activities as brand expansion and sub-branding, in the quest for high market share. (H.C.)

See also: *gentei, okyaku*

madogiwazoku

窓際族

Corporate deadwood

There is a sub-group within Japanese companies consisting of redundant, or uncooperative employees who, instead of being dismissed, are relegated to a position of virtually no importance or responsibilities. They are referred to as *madogiwazoku*, literally meaning "window seat clan." *madogiwazoku* workers are a common facet of most companies. If an employee has shown themselves to be unreliable, they will often be assigned to a new position that has a vastly decreased workload—often to the extent that they may basically sit by a window with nothing to do all day.

It has become a virtual matter of fact in many economies that employees who are uncooperative, unreliable, or not entirely necessary, will be terminated. Most contracts last for a set period of time and breach of contract can easily lead to demotion or being fired. But unlike their Western counterparts, most Japanese companies still hire employees for life. Once an employee is hired, no matter how poorly they work or how badly they fit in, a company will be very hesitant to fire them. It might be thought that this security would encourage workers to be lazy; but this is not the case. In the Japanese work culture, where group identity is used to judge a person's worth, being lazy and useless can lead to non-inclusion and disdain from fellow workers. (T.C.)

See also: *giri, ippanshoku, kaisha, keiyaku, shūshin koyō, salaryman*

manga

漫画

Comic

The modern Japanese comic was born after World War II, but its history is very complex, with examples of artwork that influenced the development of modern Japanese comics dating from as early as the 11th century.

The word *manga*, literally translated, means "whimsical pictures," and could be seen as the counterpart of the Western cartoon. The term *mangaka* denotes the author of *manga*, as well as a scenarist and animator. *Manga* are seen everywhere—in caricatures in the press, comic books, animated series, and the arts. This feature of Japanese culture has spread across the whole world and is highly appreciated in many countries.

The exaggerated representations found on temple walls from the early 11th century bear a similarity to modern *manga*; in the 1600s similar pictures started to be drawn on wood blocks. But *manga* didn't see significant growth until after the bombing of Nagasaki and Hiroshima. Subsequent to this, Osamu Tezuka created one of the most popular *manga* characters, called Mighty Atom (Astro Boy). Tezuka, who is known in Japan as the "God of Manga," made his comic book debut in 1947 with New Treasure Island, which sold 400,000 copies. During the 1960s, as the original manga generation grew up, people no longer viewed it as something to be enjoyed only by children. From 1980 onwards *manga* saw an evolution in genre and style, and also the introduction of sophisticated techniques specifically geared toward enhancing its looks and effects. Many successful artists, such as Fujiko Fujio (Doraemon), Matsumoto Leiji (Starblazers), Toriyama Akira (Dragon Ball), Rumiko Takahashi (Ranma 1⁄2), Takehiko Inoue (Slam Dunk), and Masashi Kishimoto (Naruto), have followed in the footsteps of Tezuka to contribute to this lucrative and popular entertainment industry.

The Japanese publishing market is one of the most vigorous in the world. The gross sales of digital manga 171 million yen, the sales of physical manga 166 billion yen in 2017.

The *manga* comic books usually follow the traditional style found in Japan, being read from right to left, the opposite of American and European books. The fans of *manga* have made sure that many *manga* produced abroad today are in the traditional Japanese style, collected in small volumes which appear like small books. In Japan, *manga* is first published in magazines as a collection of different stories, and if certain ones become really popular then the stories are selected and published in a new volume.

Different kinds of *manga* have developed, each with its own title. The five main types are *shōnen* (for boys), *shōjo* (for girls), *seinen* (for men), *josei* (for women), and finally *kodomo* (for children).

manga has seen phenomenal success in recent years, not only in Japan, but also in other countries, where it is steadily growing in popularity and influence and *manga* artwork has begun to influence artists all over the world. Initially, the *manga* wave made its way only gradually into foreign markets, first in association with animated series and then independently. European publishers also translated *manga* into German, Italian, Dutch, French, and other languages. Today the main exports of *manga* are either children's television or *manga* films for a more select audience, whereas in Japan *manga* is still used in the form of paper cartoons, and for purposes other than entertainment. A guide to economics has been printed in *manga*, as are magazines targeted at all age groups. (M.E.)

See also: *otaku, wakon yōsai*

marugakae

丸抱え

Being absorbed in one's company

The term *marugakae* refers to the state of being absorbed in one's company, resulting in a total dedication of the employee to the firm. *marugakae* can also be translated as completely financed, sponsored, or under patronage. The expression has deep roots in Japanese history, tradition, and culture. In ancient Japan, *marugakae* was the attitude expected for *geisha* and personal servants in their relationship to the landlord.

In Japanese labor relations, there is a connection between private and professional life. The company offers protection to its employees who are proud to be members of the enterprise. The company may be referred to as a (second) family, in which the employee is completely involved. The concept of *marugakae* signifies identification, loyalty, and an emotional bond between person and corporation. Unlike in Western management, individual goals and a company's objectives go hand-in-hand. Despite the strict hierarchical structure of a Japanese company, employees accept their position and field of activities.

marugakae is potentially a win-win situation for both company and employee: in exchange for loyalty the employer offers a wide range of material and psychological rewards. Satisfied employees are good for business. In order to ensure employee satisfaction—and thus loyalty—Japanese companies emphasize promotion opportunities, long-term development, continuous training, and job security. Lifetime employment and promotion by seniority play a major role in Japanese Human Resource Management. *marugakae* is also connected to the Japanese group spirit. Once a person becomes a member of a group, he or she is required to show that they are a full and integral player in the team.

marugakae has a strong influence on the Japanese working style. For example, a Japanese office is significantly different from a Western one. People share a room with closely spaced desks. In the workplace there is not much space for privacy, employees work together as a team, and business issues are discussed together. However, supervision is strict, because you share the same room with your superiors. The layout of a Japanese office reinforces the image of a company that absorbs its employees.

Japanese employees tend to work overtime. The term *salaryman* was created to describe a male Japanese employee who works hard for his company from dawn till dusk. A typical *salaryman* spends his whole working life, and also a major part of his free time, at the same company. While *marugakae* reflects a way of motivating employees and realizing that they are the core intellectual capital of a business, it also comes with several problems, including tragic cases of *karōshi*—death from overwork. (M.F.)

See also: *nenkō joretsu, salaryman, shūshin koyō, karōshi*

meishi

名刺

Business Card

Just as in the West, the standard modern format of the Japanese business card (*meishi*) is 90×55 mm, and they contain essentially the same information. Depending on context, they might have an English and a Japanese version on either side. Unlike the occidental equivalent, *meishi* are usually plainer in their format, quite standardized, and constitute a formalized rite of the business etiquette.

In accordance with the traditional Japanese way of introducing oneself, the *meishi* states the company/organization's name first in the largest characters. Then come the person's division/title, surname, and given name. If the holder of the card is from Japan, his name will be written in *kanji* (Japanese ideograms) and might include a *furigana* (basic Japanese syllable-based writing system) legend of the name's pronunciation if it is composed of little-known characters.

On the right side of the card, e-mail address, telephone/fax number, and other relevant contact information is displayed. Contrary to the Western format, the order in which the address of the individual is presented goes from general to specific: The Japanese standard for writing an address starts with the country and postal code, then the prefecture name, ward, city, district, building name, building number, and finally room/office number.

In a business context, *meishi* are exchanged when introducing oneself for the first time. *meishi* are usually kept in a protective case, as their fresh appearance must reflect that of the beholder. When presenting one's card to another party, it should be held at the top corners and shown so that the receiver may read the giver's information immediately and grab the card at the two bottom corners. The words *choudai-itashimasu* normally accompany the presentation of the card, at which point both parties bow to each other. If a person of lower standing exchanges cards with one of higher status, the subordinate is to bow longer and lower and should hand the card lower than that of the superior. Following the presentation of the information on one's card, the company name, division/title, and name should be spoken—in this order. If receiving a card, it should be carefully considered, handled gently, information on the card should be immediately memorized, and note should be taken of the giver's standing. Following the introductory conversation, the *meishi* should be gently laid on a table and kept in front of oneself or inserted at the back of a card-filer if parting with the giver.

There are certain behaviors which if displayed during the process of exchanging *meishi* would generally be taken as insults. Some notorious examples are namely: folding a card in two, placing the card in one's pocket, receiving the card with one hand, placing one's fingers over a name or other information on the card, not bowing when receiving the card, not reading the card when it is received, not remembering the name and having to read it off the card afterwards, writing on the card, or using the card to fan oneself, pick one's teeth, or in some other playful mannerism.

Other actions, although they may not be regarded as direct insults, are to be avoided as they might be viewed as clumsy: for instance, presenting one's card with the name upside down (from the point of view of the receiver) or presenting the English side up to a Japanese speaker. Not placing the card on the table in an orderly fashion might also prick the sensitivity of the person who gives it, as it would suggest that the receiver does not know how to treat the giver tidily and with respect.

As a rule of thumb, it is safest to remember that the *meishi* represents one's standing, achievements, pride, and identity. It is thus to be handled accordingly, with similar respect to that which the person in question deserves—which implies sensitivity, attention to detail, and devotion. (P.G.)

See also: *kaisha, kanji*

muda – muri - mura

無理 - 無駄 - ムラ

Different Types of Waste

muda-muri-mura are the three types of waste identified in the legendary Toyota Production System, also known as the Toyota Way. The Toyota Way is a management philosophy that expresses the values and rules of conduct embraced by all Toyota employees. It is based on respect for people and continuous improvement, summed up in five keywords: challenge, *kaizen* (continuous improvement), *genchi genbutsu* (現地弁物), respect, and teamwork.

muda is a traditional Japanese term for waste that doesn't add value to the customer but does consume resources. This is a key concept in the Toyota Production System, since eliminating waste is a way to increase profitability. In most production systems, only a small fraction of total time and effort actually adds value for the customer. The key to eliminating waste efficiently would be to clearly define what the value is in a specific product from a customer's perspective, and then remove the non-value activities step by step.

As identified by Toyota's chief engineer, Taiichi Ohno, there are seven wastes in the production system. The first waste is *overproduction*, that is, producing more than the customer requires. Traditional mass production is a good example of overproduction, because production continues irrespective of the quantity ordered by the customer, increasing the amount of space needed for storing raw materials as well as the finished goods. The second waste is *unnecessary transportation*, which includes multiple handling and delay in handling, since every time a product is moved there is a risk of it being damaged, lost, or delayed. The third waste is *inventory*, which is the purchasing of unnecessary raw materials regarding both work in progress and finished works. The fourth is *motion*, which refers to actions by the producer or equipment that is not productive and hence does not add value. The fifth waste is *defects*, meaning that part of the production requires reworking; this includes extra costs for reworking the part and rescheduling production. The sixth waste is *over-processing*, which are unnecessary steps or work procedures; this includes overly complex and expensive tools. The seventh waste is *time*, which refers to delays: whenever goods are not being processed, time is being wasted.

muri is a traditional Japanese term for overburdening, and is the second waste identified in the Toyota Way. *muri* happens when processes and operators do not have sufficient time to carry out their work, so affecting the whole flow. Overburdening of workers is considered a waste because it leads to inefficiency and consequently problems with safety and quality. At the same time, overburdening of equipment causes breakdowns and defects.

mura is a traditional Japanese term for unevenness and occurs when products are batched together and pushed through a production plant. A widely varying workload is a waste, since it has a direct impact on the productivity of employees and the materials they use. To ease the burden, jobs can be broken down into other tasks. In most companies, there is also the *mura* of people pushing themselves harder at the end of reporting periods in an effort to boost their output. This causes sales to write too many orders, and makes equipment and employees work too hard in order to meet the deadline. This performance of the job without proper planning leads to overburdening, which is *muri*. *mura* thus creates *muri*, which makes it even harder to eliminate *muda*.

In order to achieve the goal of eliminating *muda-muri-mura* in the Toyota production system, Taiichi Ohno had to further elaborate the celebrated Just-in-Time management system. JIT was already efficient in the way that materials were delivered to the right place, at the right time, in the right amount; but to take the next step Ohno realized that quality had to be controlled as well. He reflected that he could apply *jidōka* (self-regulation), which would automatically stop the production line where a defective product was found. At each worksite, groups were formed to discuss the best way of doing this, and Ohno constantly had these words in mind: **Eliminate *muda-muri-mura* completely**. Out of these discussions, a *kanban* system was established, which also involved improving communication via the Andon system—whereby pulling a chord enabled workers to stop the entire production line if a problem occurred. The *kanban* (看板) system is a pull production control, in which materials are released into production only when they are needed. This development was the result of the *kaizen* (continuous improvement) in which all the workers at Toyota took part. (J.G.)

See also: *ba (genba)*, *jidōka* (*andon*), Just-in-time (JIT), *kaizen*, *kanban*, 5S-System *naitei*

内定

Job confirmation

naitei is an important aspect of the intricacies of hiring within Japanese business. Literally speaking, it is a job confirmation and can be directly translated as an "unofficial offer" or "tentative decision." However, the direct translation can be misleading, especially to those schooled in the West. When a prospective employee is offered *naitei* it is done in an informal manner such as by e-mail or telephone, but even though the official documented job offer is written at a much later date, companies are required to hire candidates to whom they have given a notification of *naitei*. Exceptions can only be made in extremely rare circumstances, such as in cases where the candidate has falsified information or is no longer suitable to work as designated. *naitei* is in effect a binding agreement. It is only offered for full-time employment, and usually refers to lifetime employment, which is still the most common way in Japan for new graduates to be hired.

naitei is an important feature in the job-hunting process for the Japanese university student. Job-hunting in Japan is called *shushoku katsudō*, and is a much more systematic process than in the West. Students in Japanese universities begin the job-hunting process in the beginning of their 3rd year, usually with corporate internships. During the second semester (starting in September) they begin attending regular job fairs and information sessions. At the end of their 3rd year students begin going to interviews and taking company examinations. Then in the first semester of the final year students begin to receive their confirmation notices or *naitei*. This is usually between April and July, long before they will sign their official confirmation notice in October. The *naitei* is thus given nearly a year before the candidate starts working. Job candidates are bound to work for a company once they have accepted the *naitei*.

The *naitei* reflects the way the Japanese do business. Although it is not a documented offer, it is in some ways more important than the official appointment. In Japanese business many agreements are not documented at first and are only verbal. Westerners sometimes regard the *naitei* as unimportant precisely because it is not official, but in Japan it counts as a legitimate contractual agreement even though not explicitly written down.

In recent years some students have received multiple *naitei* because of the retiring baby-boomer population. In these cases, students must accept one offer and cannot change their decision once they have accepted. After accepting *naitei* it is common practice for company personnel—usually former alumni of the schools from which the students will graduate—to take the new hire out for lunch or dinner.

This process makes the beginning of the students' fourth year of university very stressful. Not only is there tremendous pressure on students from companies to prove themselves worthy of a position, but there is also pressure from parents. Students will feel shamed and families will be embarrassed if their children do not receive *naitei*. This creates another issue for students, because they will either have to start the job-hunting process all over again, or accept a position that may be lower in status.

The formality of the processes of job hiring in Japan can create difficulties for students who do not follow the standard Japanese university system. Students who take a leave of absence or who study abroad and are not awarded full credits may have to stay in school longer than fellow students. In cases when a student is scheduled to graduate in the first semester of the school year, jobs will not be available once they graduate. This is usually not the case in the West, in which job offers and hiring happen all year round (although in the West there are high times for hiring as well). Japanese students in this situation are usually forced to take another semester of classes. This is often the case when Japanese university students have graduated from foreign high school systems such as the United States', in which the school year begins in the fall. These students are often inclined to take four and half years of undergraduate studies in order to leave no gaps between the time they graduate and the time they begin work. (J.R.G.)

See also: *jirei, seishan, shushoku katsudō, gakubatsu*

naniwabushi

浪花節

Emotion-drenched personal appeal

naniwabushi is a tactic in Japanese business negotiations, in which one party makes an emotion-drenched personal appeal to remind the negotiation parties of their status and responsibilities within the social order. The party with lower status adopts the position of a victim, the goal being to generate empathy within the negotiation process. By showing vulnerability instead of becoming aggressive, the lower status party gives his opponent an opportunity to be generous and show his humanity. This creates a comfortable negotiation atmosphere and avoids disputes.

The idea of *naniwabushi* derives from narrative chants which originated in the 5th century, then sung by itinerant entertainers and later revived during the Tokugawa Shogunate, which concerned the sad plight of broken love, separated families, and tragic heroics. Revived in the form of *naniwabushi*, the process can be divided into three stages:

kikkake: The first stage provides general background information, including an introduction to the people involved, describing their thoughts and feelings. Here, the negotiator communicates his good feelings about the long-term relationship.

seme: In the second stage the negotiator reports on the critical incidents. Here he has to present all the events that have made the situation difficult, highlighting the efforts he has made, and underscoring that his recovery is dependent on the acceptance of his request.

urei: The last stage includes the final request. After giving detailed and apologetic explanations of the causes, it is important to show great sorrow, pathos, and self-pity to persuade his opponent to be benevolent. Here the negotiator usually explains in a more comprehensive way the consequences that will ensue if his request is turned down. This stage is marked by an atmosphere of melodrama in order to be as persuasive as possible.

It can be difficult to understand the concept of *naniwabushi* from a Westerner's point of view, since it is based more upon emotional feelings than objective reasons. In comparison, the Western way is based on analysis, reason, and logic, beginning with an assessment of the requests made by both negotiation partners, and only followed by an explanation if considered necessary. Westerners may consider *naniwabushi* as very melodramatic and calculated.

From the Japanese perspective, *naniwabushi* reflects the fact that the group is more important than the individual. A tragic and melodramatic atmosphere makes it easier to forget contracts or commitments, and so avoids disputes and secures harmony. (C.G.)

See also: *nemawashi, enryo, wa*

nemawashi
根回し
Informal consultation

In gardening, *nemawashi* means digging out the earth around a plant before it is transplanted. In business, it means caring about relationships, holding preliminary negotiations, or trying to reach a consensus. It may also be used as a verb—*ne mawashi (w)o suru*—which can carry the deeper meaning of setting the framework and the basis for the negotiation of a special project.

nemawashi is used in the business world to describe the common habit of getting consensus before the real decision is made. All involved parties will participate in the consensus-building process. In a Western company upper management would normally decide on any change, which would then have to be accepted by the other employees. But given the traditional Japanese accent on harmony, their manner of decision-making is more bottom-up than top-down. Of course it takes more time, but afterwards everyone accepts the decision, since they also took part in the process, and the actual accomplishment of the change decided upon can be carried out much more quickly, as everyone already knows the details.

The actual process can be described as follows. First, all relevant parties (whether individuals, groups, or companies) are asked their thoughts on the topic being discussed. They are asked to give their feedback and support. If someone is not willing to join in the consensus, he might experience soft pressure from the rest of group. The consensus is arrived at by majority reflection supported by the respect which lower-standing persons pay to the more powerful and influential.

Sometimes *nemawashi* between different companies may occur together with giving presents and inviting the business partner to a meal or to a *nomikai*—which from a Western perspective can seem close to bribery. But since such things are common in Japanese business culture, in fact they are just one more aspect of the pursuit of harmony and care for the other in business relations. (M.H.)

See also: hanseikai, ningen kankei, ringi-system, *wa, senpai - kōhai*

nengajō - shochumimai
年賀状 - 暑中見舞い
Greetings

nengajō and *shochumimai* are types of postcards used as traditional seasonal greetings. Generally, the *nengajō* is sent at the end of the year to arrive on New Year itself, in order to wish the receiver a happy New Year, and express gratitude for the previous year and hope that the good relationship might continue. *shochumimai* is sent at the hottest time of the year to ask about the receiver's health. Receivers of these greeting cards are usually relatives, friends, and people from the same company. *nengajō* and *shochumimai* are similar to the Christmas card in Western countries, and they show that the writer really cares about the receivers. Each is sent only once a year, but they are intended to build on a good relationship which plays an important role in a person's life.

The tradition of *nengajō* is said have started around the 7th century, during Heian period. Before postcards became the standard form of *nengajō*, the New Year greeting was written as a letter and delivered by express messenger to people who lived far away. In the beginning, few New Year greeting letters were sent, but after postcards were invented, more people started to send such cards and the *nengajō* became popular. Today most Japanese, from children to adults, send *nengajō* for the New Year, and in 2005 over 45 billion postcards for *nengajō* were issued. A general *nengajō* includes sentences of greeting and an illustration of the Oriental zodiac for that year. The purpose of *nengajō* is to hail a happy New Year, but one should not send *nengajō* to someone in *mochu*, or in mourning, because he or she cannot celebrate the New Year right after losing a relative. In advance of the New Year, the person in mourning is expected to send postcards to people who are close to them informing them of the situation.

The history of *shochumimai* dates back to around the Edo period. In the past, the Japanese divided the year into two periods, and sent greetings for the beginning of each. The first greeting was for New Year, and the second was called *shochumimai*. After postcards became standardized, the number of people sending *shochumimai* increased. A typical *shochumimai* includes words that express care for the receiver's health in a hot summer, and often a drawing or a picture that is associated with a cool, refreshing feeling. The specific date for when *shochumimai* should be delivered is not established, but it is supposed to arrive after the rainy season but before *risshu* (立秋), the Japanese term for the first day of autumn. A greeting card that is sent to arrive after *risshu* is called *zansho mimai* (残暑見舞い). *shochumimai* is not sent as frequently as *nengajō*, because the New Year is considered a bigger event than the start of summer, but still it is an important custom through which the Japanese show concern and respect to the receivers.

In December, preprinted and prestamped postcards can be bought in every post office. These postcards include a lottery number, of which the winning number is announced some days after New Year. Prizes, though, are not of money as in a normal lottery, but goods such as bicycles and televisions. There are also lottery numbers on some postcards for *shochumimai* too, but not as frequently as for *nengajō* postcards. *shochumimai* is sent less often than *nengajō*. *nengajō* postcards must be brought to the post offices before December 26, in order for them to be collected and delivered for the first hours of the new year. Postcards which have not been received by the post office by December 26 will be delivered as normal mail.

Although many people still use postcards for *nengajō* and *shochumimai*, the number of people who actually write such greetings is becoming smaller because of the spread of the Internet and printing software. Through computers and cell phones, messages with a creative design can easily be sent, and thus there is less need for postcards. Printing software allows users to print out decorated and (pre-addressed postcards simply by choosing from various patterns. However, in business and other formal contexts, actual handwriting is appreciated since the effort shows how much the sender cares about the receiver. The printing software can still be used, but often there are hand-written personal comments in the spaces provided. (K.H.)

See also: *oseibo/ochūgen*

nenkō joretsu

年功序列

Promotion by seniority

In many Japanese corporations, full-time employees (*seishain* or 正社員) are promoted on a strictly annual basis or upon the retirement of an older worker. This system is called *nenkō joretsu*, promotion by seniority— a term combining the two words *nenkō* ("long service" or "seniority") and *joretsu* ("hierarchy" or "ranking system"), and sometimes rendered in Western texts as the *nenkō System*. Unlike the standard Western system, promotions in *nenkō joretsu* are not always merit-based.

The *nenkō System* fits Japan's cultural structure, wherein seniority must be respected. However, while in wider society seniority would be determined by age, in the *nenkō System* seniority is determined by the year of entry into a company. This would mean that an employee aged twenty-six who has worked for the company for only two years, would be junior to a co-worker in the same department who is twenty-five but has worked for the company for four years.

There are many benefits to the *nenkō System*. For instance: both employees and employers know when promotions are coming and are better able to plan and budget for the future of both the individual and company. It also facilitates the common practice of periodically placing workers in different departments, enabling them to develop all-round knowledge of the company, and in turn generating loyalty between employee and employer. Additionally, because pay rises occur yearly, this system conforms to the social structure by channeling benefits to those who are financially more in need: younger employees tend to be unmarried and need less money to support themselves, while older employees are married with children. Some companies even offer benefits to help pay for the tuition of employees' children. In this system employees are also less likely to change company—out of fear of losing their current status upon leaving the current employer—and in turn employees become very future-oriented and believe that if they stay with the company, they will have financial stability in the future.

Recently, this system has come under scrutiny. One of the primary problems for the *nenkō System* is Japan's aging population. As the Japanese become older and older, companies that implement the *nenkō System* have ever greater financial responsibilities for their retired employees: the financial burden of retirement money rests on the younger employees and the company's expenses become ever larger.

Another disadvantage of this system relates to *hiseikikoyōusha* (非正規雇用者), non-full-time workers. With the recession, a trend has emerged for companies to hire temporary workers, who do not fit into the *nenkō System* and are not given the same benefits as life employees. This issue has been the cause of much debate within Japanese society.

The *nenkō System* also leads to a lack of specialists within a company. The system itself is designed to enable companies to give each worker all-round experience, but while this gives each worker the ability to do many different jobs and is an effective "cover" system for when an employee takes time off, it also prevents employees from becoming true specialists in any field. Additionally, when a specialist is needed, a company must hire an outsider, which may itself disrupt the hierarchy.

The *nenkō System* has led to instances in which employees do not exert themselves, because they know they will be promoted nonetheless. When a star worker emerges within a company, while his skill may be recognized and highly commended, his salary will not necessarily reflect the contribution he makes. Such workers nowadays are tending to change employers in search of more responsibility and higher salaries. (W.H.)

See also: *haichi tenkan, kaisha, seishain*

ningen kankei - jinmyaku
人間関係 - 人脈
Human relationships

ningen kankei is translated as "human relationships," and the term emphasizes group harmony. In business contexts it refers to the relationships of workers within and outside the company.

ningen kankei is considered very important and is deeply rooted in Japanese culture. It originates from Japan's village-based culture, which emphasized cooperation amongst members of the group, the following of rules, and working together, rather than acting in individuals' own self-interest. A related term is *shudan shugi* or "group orientation," which places greater importance on group goals and members acting as one, rather than on personal goals. Japanese culture puts emphasis on *wa* ("harmony") when working in a group, in order to work cooperatively together. Avoiding violations of *wa* is very important in remaining part of the group, otherwise a person will be treated as an outcast. This is to be avoided at all costs, given that most of the group members will live and work together for their entire lives. Maintaining positive *ningen kankei* with others and remaining a part of the group was essential to living in the Japanese village system, and this has shaped contemporary Japanese company culture.

Many Japanese companies still retain *sūshin koyō* (終身雇用), the lifetime employment system, which results in workers placing greater importance on *ningen kankei*. *sūshin koyō* ensures that workers have employment until their retirement, as a reward for loyalty to the company. By following this system, most workers continue their career in one company, since they have a secure job. Therefore, to keep their job and to maintain a comfortable workplace, building and developing *ningen kankei* with other workers becomes crucial.

ningen kankei is also important outside the firm. "Building relationships inside and outside the company" is termed making *jinmyaku* (人脈) and refers to people who exert a positive influence and give good advice. *jinmyaku* can be developed in a variety of contexts, such as a group of graduates from the same university, those born and raised in the same city, those that have the same hobbies, experts in a field unfamiliar to the individual seeking advice, and so on. Japanese culture considers a person who has a wide *jinmyaku* as a person who can get along with people with completely different backgrounds, vocations, and ages. By having wide *jinmyaku*, a person is able to obtain information as quickly as possible, and to get help when in need.

In order to build and develop *ningen kankei*, it is necessary to attend extra activities outside of work such as a "drinking event," termed *nomikai*, or a "company trip," called *shain ryoko*, for all employees. *nomikai* is the traditional Japanese drinking party and provides a chance to get to know colleagues better, and to talk more frankly under the influence of alcohol. There used to be a tacit agreement that everyone must attend *nomikai*, and this is still adhered to in many companies, although the strictness of the attendance rule varies. Japanese culture considers *ningen kankei* more important than achievement. Therefore, a person who can maintain group harmony is valued more than one who has the capability to finish a task by himself. *nomikai* is an extension of work that can develop group harmony, and which new recruits are expected to attend in order to be known and to show their respect to their superiors.

shain ryokō (社員旅行) works in a similar way. *shain ryokō* refers to a company trip held once a year, offered to all workers, to which attendance is required. It involves workers from all departments from the company, although if the company is too big, the trip is carried out by individual departments. Thus, *shain ryokō* is a chance to get to know existing and new colleagues, and to create harmony throughout the company. (H.I.)

See also: *shūshin koyō, tateshakai, nomikai, shudan shugi, wa, shain ryoko*

nomikai

飲み会

Drinking Party

The word *nomikai*, meaning "drinking event," describes any drinking party that involves more than two people and that includes alcohol. The location of *nomikai* could be anywhere, including at home, at a restaurant, or in a park. The most popular place for *nomikai* is *izakaya* (居酒屋), a drinking establishment that serves both alcohol and food. The *izakaya* is favored by many businessmen because the price of alcohol and food is relatively inexpensive compared to bars or other restaurants.

Attendance at *nomikai* is a social obligation; unless there is a family emergency or the person is severely sick, it is mandatory for employees to attend. By attending, employees show support, respect, and gratitude towards the company and their co-workers. When a *nomikai* is for someone such as an executive, manager, or *senpai*, meaning "senior" among the workers, employees are often required to attend.

Drinking is considered as a means by which employees can interact with each other. Many people and companies in Japan believe that alcohol helps people open up and has the power to bring people together. When at a *nomikai*, employees are allowed to discuss freely and informally business and other work-related issues. With the help of the effect alcohol provides, employees build better relationships. Thus, intoxication at a *nomikai* is acceptable, if not encouraged—there is no societal stigma towards intoxicated businessmen in

Japan. While employees are at a *nomikai*, there is less tension and separation between *senpai* and *kōhai*, that is, "juniors." *kōhai* are allowed to talk more freely to their *senpai*, which is known as *bureiko*. This behavior is only allowed when they are drinking.

Communication while drinking is an important part of business in Japan. This activity is often called *nomunication*, an interlingual portmanteau term derived from *nomi-* "drinking," and "communication." *nomikai* start with a welcome speech and a toast, containing words of reflection and encouragement, and end with a *shime*, or "ending speech." These speeches are generally done by someone of the highest position, or a *kanji*, an "organizer of the gathering." The *kanji* is responsible for the preparation of *nomikai*, from choosing the location to collecting money from attendees.

nomikai is an important activity in Japanese business contexts. Company-arranged *nomikai* might be on the company expense account or could come out of the employees` own pockets. When it is not on the company's budget, attendees usually pay a set amount. Most *izakaya* have *nomi-hodai*, or an "all-you-can-drink menu," therefore, all attendees pay the same amount up front.

Many companies in Japan arrange monthly *nomikai* in the form of a *tasseikai* (達成会), an "achievement celebration party," or a *hanseikai* (反省会), a "reflection meeting." A *kangeikai* (歓迎会), or "welcome party," is held when someone new starts at the company. A *konshinkai* (懇親会), a "drinking party," usually involving employees from other companies, is held in order to facilitate employees of different companies getting to know each other. A "farewell party," or *sobetsukai* (送別会), is held when an employee is leaving work for a reason such as retirement or marriage. A *sobetsukai* is not held when an employee gets fired or quits for unexpected or negative reasons. These *nomikai*s are arranged by companies in the hope of developing camaraderie and a sense of unity among employees.

The Japanese end-of-year party, or *bonenkai* (忘年会), is a kind of *nomikai*, translated as "forgetting-the-year gathering." People get together to mark the end of the year. Though usually held in December, there is no specific date for the party, and therefore it is not unusual for them to be held in November. The *bonenkai* is one of the most important *nomikai* of the year. Some companies hold games like bingo to show appreciation to their employees for their diligence that year. The *shinnenkai* (新年会), or New Year party, is similar to the *bonenkai*, except it is held at the beginning of a year. Usually managers and executives make speeches about their plans for the year. (R.K.)

See also: *hanseikai, shimoza (kamiza), senpai/kōhai, shudan shugi (kojin shugi), wa*

okyaku
お客
Consumer(s)

The importance of the term *okyaku*, meaning "consumer," reflects the fact that Japan, with its more than 120 million highly educated consumers, is one of the largest consumer markets in the world. One in thirteen people is a professional consumer, which means they have a strong influence on other consumers and are well informed about the product, sometimes even more than the sales staff. Most Japanese consumers belong to the middle class and are quite wealthy. Japanese consumer culture developed in the beginning of the 1980s, however, average spending fell during the recession. Yet even though consumers' incomes have decreased, Japanese households are among the richest in the world.

There are several particularities about Japanese consumer behavior compared to other countries in the world. The emphasis on *shinhatsubai*, meaning "new product," and *gentei*, translated as "limited edition," provide examples of this. Products need to stay interesting to the Japanese consumer, which is why companies keep releasing new models and product improvements. Often there are small changes, for instance to the packaging, or the flavor of the product, but that in itself creates a newness and distinctive style to the brand. So as a result, products have a very short life cycle; they enter the market fast, but also disappear quickly. Another specialty of the Japanese market is the extraordinary service provided. Japanese companies pay a good deal of money to research what their customers want, and work hard to satisfy consumers' demands. Hence, they are very relationship- and communication-oriented. Even if a customer's request is illogical, the company will not say no, and will try to meet the demand. If the consumer wants a pink computer, for example, he will get it. This is probably why there are so many customer service centers in Japan. That way, companies can react fast to consumers' complaints, and improve their product.

Japanese consumers also pay great attention to the quality and safety standards of a product, as well as its appearance and packaging. Japanese consumers often reject a product if there is a scratch on the packaging. Moreover, food products must look very fresh, and vegetables for example will not be sold if the shape or color are not perfect. Usually quality comes first for the brand-oriented Japanese consumers, but they are also very price-sensitive; they inform themselves about the product and compare prices. Nowadays, they tend to emphasize price and functionality over brand or status, and Japanese consumers have learned that a high price and good quality are not necessarily synonymous. A high affinity for technology is also a particularity of the Japanese, and they are always eager to try out new things. In addition, Japanese are very brand-orientated. Consumption is often status-oriented, and global brand names are highly valued. Japan is a luxury mass market, and they love to buy goods from brands like Burberry, Louis Vuitton, or Gucci to show their status, but at the same time they are not loyal to one brand. In many cases, the corporate brand is emphasized, and not the product brand.

Several consumer groups can be identified in Japan, and companies work on responding quickly to satisfy the demands of each demographic group, and to offer tailor-made products, because these are key to building a strong customer relationship. These include the silver market, young working women and single men in their twenties to thirties, the new rich, and the *otaku*.

Because of the rapid aging of Japan's population and the fall in the fertility rate, the percentage of elderly retirees in Japan is constantly growing. This group has accumulated large sums through saving, so they have plenty of money and time to spend. They mainly spend money on travel, health, and fashion. Another influential consumer group in Japan is the baby boomers, born after World War II and about to retire. They are known as the "typical Japanese"—married, successful but not too successful, middle class, white collar workers.

Another newly established consumer group is that of single working women. They are financially independent and have a considerable income, which is often spent on luxuries such as travel, fashion, brand products, beauty, and health clubs. This group is also characterized by a new attitude towards gender roles.

The new rich can be characterized by the showing off of their wealth, and the consumption of foreign luxury items. Moreover, they tend to invest their money in riskier assets, whereas Japanese people in general are risk averse.

otaku can be roughly translated as the English word "thou." In the 1980s, it was used as a slang word for Japanese fans of *manga* and *anime*, for self-reference.

Nowadays, it refers to the consumer group that is fanatical about any number of hobbies. These can be comics and animation, electronics of all kinds, or collecting *manga*-inspired dolls. An *otaku* is usually an unmarried male, working in a technology-related field. (K.K.)

See also: *gentei, māketingu, manga, nedan*

pachinko

パチンコ

Pachinko

pachinko is a game closely resembling pinball, except that it is played vertically. The player buys a certain amount of small metal balls, which are then fed into the *pachinko* machine. The goal is to get as many balls as possible into the slots, which can then lead to big winnings at the *pachinko* parlor. The main players of *pachinko* are men in their thirties or forties, usually salesmen who come after work, although recently women players are increasing as well. For Japanese management personnel, this is a way to escape from everyday life, or to relieve stress. However, due to the gambling controversy behind *pachinko*, the game has sometimes been viewed negatively, especially in foreign contexts.

pachinko came to Japan during the Taisho period as a game called Corinth from the United States. In this game, the goal was to put a ball into a hole by hitting it with a flat stick. If the players won the game, they were rewarded with caramels or simple toys. After World War II, during which Japan was mass-producing arms, particularly in Nagoya, there were a large amount of ball bearings remaining, and these were transferred into the Japanese *pachinko* industry. As metal *pachinko* machines became more common, and technological advances came about, the old *pachinko* game gradually evolved into the metal *pachinko* game that is now rampant in Japan.

pachinko is a popular leisure activity in Japan, with roughly 50% of the Japanese population having played at least once in their life. Depending on the machine or the shop the payoff from playing *pachinko* varies. If a store has just opened, they can adjust the payoff to be at a very high rate, say 90%, to encourage players to continue to play. However, the machines could be at a lower payoff rate, say 65-70%, to stop professional *pachinko* players from winning all the earnings. On average per year, one *pachinko* machine earns about eight million yen, and if this is put on a larger scale, the revenue from all *pachinko* machines can amount to roughly 32 trillion yen. The ball bearings to play the game cost four yen, so with such low costs to play, and the occasional pay-off from winning, the game is very attractive to Japanese people.

pachinko appeals to *salarymen*, because it allows them to escape to a world where they can make active decisions, and in turn relieve stress. When playing *pachinko*, one does not have to be explicitly aware of where the balls are going inside the machine. Thus, while playing the game, one can just gaze at the machine, not really thinking of anything, which allows *salarymen* to forget about their obligations at work or at home. To play the game, one simply controls the speed at which the balls are put in, or when the balls enter the machine.

There is no time limit to *pachinko*, so people can stay there for as long as they want, without having to worry about workers telling them to hurry up and go home. Japanese *salarymen* already have enough stress at work, and they probably experience extra stress if they have an unstable family relationship, so *pachinko* is a way to escape into a world of their own, where they answer to no-one. This type of freedom is what attracts businessmen to *pachinko*.

The contemporary debate about *pachinko* centers on its close relationship to gambling. Once a player has finished playing for the night, the balls are exchanged for prizes in the *pachinko* parlor, which can then be taken to shops in the area that will exchange the prizes for money. Because the *pachinko* shop itself does not actually deal with exchanging the balls into money, the game cannot be labeled as gambling, and the police cannot force the *pachinko* parlor to shut down its business. However, it is widely known that the prizes can be exchanged for cash at shops in the area, usually run by *yakuza*. The police try to watch these areas, but otherwise the fact that pachinko is closely related to gambling does not deter Japanese people from playing the game.

pachinko is not really found in other countries outside of Asia. It will probably neither be accepted in Western countries because of the specific context of the game. (E.K.)

See also: *salaryman*

oseibo - ochūgen

お歳暮・お中元

Presents

The terms *oseibo* and *ochūgen* both refer to "gifts" in the context of the gift-giving tradition called *okurimono* (贈り物). The Japanese etiquette for gift-giving is a tradition with a very long history and is universally valued. The presents are aimed at friends, relatives, acquaintances, persons one has become indebted to, and business partners. The importance of this tradition for upholding relationships and business contacts can therefore not be underestimated. As along with the tradition comes a good deal of important etiquette and expectations, it is a fairly complex topic that has led to the creation of a whole industry in Japan.

Of the vast number of occasions on which it is expected that people give presents in Japan, the two seasonal presents called *oseibo* and *ochūgen* bear a special importance. The *ochūgen* is a midsummer gift traditionally given during *obon*, "the festival of the dead." The tradition originates in Taoism, which has a ceremonial day on July the 15th on the lunar calendar, which happens to be the Buddhist festival Bon (*ura-bon*). When Taoism came into contact with Buddhism, the tradition changed from offering a present to the dead, to presenting a gift to an indebted person. Though the tradition remained, the time when these gifts are given changed to a period between 1–15 July on the solar calendar. The recipients of these *ochūgen*-gifts are usually relatives, *nakōdo* (仲人) or "matchmakers," physicians or doctors, teachers, and superiors, or customers in the company. However, this list is not complete, and one has to decide for himself if he feels indebted to a person.

The budget spent for the *ochūgen* ranges somewhere between 2,000 to 100,000 yen and is determined according to the level of association with the recipient. Nowadays it usually averages around 3,000 yen. Like the budget, the sort of present varies from person to person. However, with the creation of an industry that helps people deal with the very exhausting and difficult process of choosing, packing, and sending the gifts, a trend towards *sanchokuhin* (差直品), meaning "commodity or goods that are sent directly from the producer or producer's shop or factory," has been established.

The *oseibo*, like the *ochūgen*, is a seasonal gift presented to persons one has become indebted to. A greater proportion of people will present *oseibo* between 1–20 December on the solar calendar. Some people, however, like to present these gifts between December 26th and January 7th, which makes them *onenga*—御年賀 or "the greeting that celebrates the New Year." While the gifts themselves and the addressees are similar to the *ochūgen*, the budget, though again ranging widely, averages this time at around 5,000 yen.

For both occasions many Japanese prefer to give seasonal gifts, and ones that can be consumed by the recipient. It is therefore common for people to present each other with food/fruit baskets, beer/sake gift boxes, or sweets. However, whatever they give, it will always be neatly packaged and expensive looking.

Since these represent just two out of many occasions on which presents are given, there are many other different matters of etiquette to consider. For the Japanese, in many cases, gifts are used to assess the value of a relationship. It is not unusual for the value of the gift, where it was bought, and how carefully and neatly it was packaged, to become of greater importance than the gift itself. That is why the convenience of the *sanchokuhin* has led to a flourishing business for companies offering these services, with a market totaling an estimated annual value of 70 billion US dollars.

Another important aspect of gift-giving therefore is the *okaeshi*, a "return gift." Though it is not explicitly prescribed, it is expected that one answers the gift with a return gift of similar value. Since this has great importance to the consistency of relations, many Japanese people keep an account of what gifts they gave, and received, and what value these had. (M.Ko.)

See also: *depāto, nengajō – shochumimmai*

ringi-seido

稟議

Group-decision making process

The *ringi-seido* is a managerial decision-making process that is used by Japanese companies (*kaisha* or 会社). The main idea behind the *ringi* process revolves around the centralized format for decision-making within a Japanese company. The main goal of using the *ringi* system is to build a consensus from all company staff members that would be affected before making any formal decision. Unlike Western companies, the *ringi* system's strength as a viable decision-making method relies on the lower or middle level of management. While many Western firms have a top to bottom system, the *ringi* system utilizes the exact opposite, where a business plan or proposal starts at the lower levels as opposed to the upper levels of management. The responsibility then lies at all levels of management, as the plan or proposal must pass through each level of management as it works its way up for the top brass to see. This method will thus involve most staff members in the decision-making process.

The actual origin of the *ringi* system is a debatable but nonetheless noteworthy detail. It is believed by some that the *ringi* system was already in practice during the feudal age of the Tokugawa period in the 17th century. Whether or not this is true, it has been recognized that the *ringi* system was first introduced as a management method in government offices, as well as national enterprises during the Meiji Era (1868-1912). The significance of its actual origins is closely connected to the anthropological importance of relationships among the Japanese people (*ningen kankei*). Arguably the strongest point of the *ringi* system is its ability to take advantage of one of Japan's oldest traditions of *shudan shugi* or "group orientation." As it requires participation from many if not most members of a company, it is easy to see that this system of involving everyone to create a better sense of unity derives from the deep-seated traditional belief that being a part of a group or organization and maintaining high levels of commitment are of the utmost importance.

The following is a brief example that demonstrates the main protocol of the *ringi* system. An idea or business plan is first conceived by member of the lower management section, and is usually discussed among co-workers. Permission will then be required from higher superiors to actually begin the *ringi* process. Upon approval, the plan must then pass through each lower-level sector and receive approval from most, if not all other co-workers, before being sent to their immediate superior. Their superior will then decide whether or not to accept the proposal, by either sending it up to the next sector of management as a form of approval, or back down to the co-workers for further adjustments until it is deemed acceptable. This process will continue until the proposal, including any and all adjustments that were made, finally reaches the top, where the head executives will also give their blessing or decide it needs further work.

To describe the *ringi* system as a purely bottom-up process would be an oversimplification, however. There are rules that govern how the company should start and conduct the *ringi*. As stated above, the proposed business plan, known as the *ringi-sho*, the paper or formal version of a business plan or document, starts from the lower or bottom levels of management, where non-formal discussions are to take place regarding the actual plan. This form of conversation or discussion is known in Japanese as *nemawashi* and plays a significant role in the development of the plan. *nemawashi* is a vital aspect of informing other co-workers and tends to occur before and during the actual *ringi* procedure. Although the birth of the plan is to take place at the bottom, the actual initiation of a *ringi* is launched from the upper levels of management. Although they will not actually see or know the details of the plan, the top management team is usually the one who decides to start the *ringi* process. From the lower levels of management, the *ringi-sho* must then be received by the head of the group, who will then forward it to the section head of the next department. If any group or department head does not agree to the stated plan, it will then be sent back down to the original lower sector, where it must be altered or re-created, and then once again it will be allowed on its journey back towards the top. Along the way the *ringi-sho* must receive an official stamp of approval from each head of department or sector before it can move on its way up.

Besides ensuring commitment from all levels of a company, the *ringi* system verifies that most members have a concrete and even extensive understanding of the company. By requiring everyone to contemplate the contents of the proposed plan, staff members will feel inclined to implement their own thoughts and ideas. This will demonstrate their knowledge of the company and ability to devise any possible improvements that will ultimately help the company or organization. It is also important to note that by having a plan move from the bottom to the top, and going through virtually all sectors of the company, fewer variables or factors will be overlooked.

Naturally, disadvantages can at times cloud the overall effectiveness of instituting the *ringi* system. The first and most evident disadvantage is the time burden. The actual process of conducting a *ringi* tends to take an extended period of time. This of course is a significant pitfall in specific scenarios where a quick decision is necessary. The other major drawback of the *ringi* system is the obscured sense of responsibility. Due to the fact that the actual proposal is started by an employee with little actual responsibility, and must pass through a multitude of superiors, the actual responsibility for decision-making along each step of the way is unclear. For this reason, the actual blame or source of responsibility tends to go unnoticed in the event of a serious error, and most are able to escape the situation unharmed, and the blunder therefore remains unaccounted for.

The *ringi* system continues to be a critical feature in most Japanese companies. As would be expected, the system does differ slightly between companies and organizations, and has seen some alterations since it was first implemented in the Meiji Era. The length of time required, along with the excessive formality involved, have been criticized as being too inefficient in the modern business world. While some scholars believe that the traditional sense of the *ringi* system is fading, the underlying purpose and philosophy of the system have proven enduring, and preserve the Japanese cultural concept of a strong, stable unit. (E.KR.)

See also: *kaisha, nemawashi, ningen kankei, shudan shugi*

ristora

リストラ

Restructuring (the Japanese economy)

ristora refers to the economic reforms implemented after the Japanese financial bubble burst, in order to recover from subsequent recession and stagflation. In 1994, the government started to instigate regulatory reforms to stimulate economic recovery. The goal of these reforms was to deregulate Japanese markets, which had been under different restrictions, prohibitions, and taxes, and to move from state-led growth, where government intervention and protection was extensive, to market-led growth, with its higher level of efficiency and lesser government intervention. The implementation of these reforms started in December 1996.

One of the most important reforms in Japan included the deregulation of the financial sector, modeled after London's "Big Bang" deregulation. These reforms aimed to provide more alternatives for investors andborrowers, improve the competitiveness of Japanese financial institutions, increase the performance of these institutions, and to enhance the transparency of corporations. The financial deregulation by the Japanese government opened up more options for investors and borrowers by allowing over-the-counter securities derivatives, selling options on individual stock, and largely removing control over foreign exchange.

To make Japanese financial institutions more competitive, the boundary between insurance companies and banks was almost removed. This meant that securities firms and insurance companies could enter the banking sector through subsidiaries, and banks would be able to go into the insurance business. The government also removed the monopoly power of the financial companies, so that independent investment groups were able to compete more freely in Japan. It also revised the guidance for pension funds for investment companies from a detailed code of conduct to a more general one. In addition, to improve Japanese markets' performance, restrictions on exchange trading were abolished.

The Japanese government also took steps to enhance the transparency and accountability of financial firms in Japan. These included classifying loans into four different categories of reliability, having outside auditors examine these classifications, and establishing a new method for calculating the sufficiency ratios for banks. It also established a consolidated method of reporting, and revised accounting standards closer to IASC International Accounting Standards. In addition, fair trade rules to protect investors were issued, and agencies for dealing with bad loans were established. Government infrastructure was amended to support this increasing surveillance.

Regarding the labor market, the Japanese government has preserved the rights of full-time employees, making it still difficult to dismiss employees. But it has further deregulated the movement of dispatch (temporary) workers, giving companies more freedom in hiring dispatch workers to fit the economic situation. This deregulation has also made it possible for private companies to provide temporary workers to companies. Furthermore, the Japanese government has given more freedom for employers to decide about the working hours and compensation of the employees, as well as their contracts. Additionally, the Equal Employment Opportunity Act has been revised by reducing protection for female workers.

The Japanese government has been more successful in deregulating and enhancing competition in some sectors than in others. Reforms in the telecommunications, electricity, large retail stores, gasoline imports, and financial services sectors have been the most successful. There has also been some enhancement in the efficiency of comprehensive licenses and permits. Furthermore, the government has revised the anti-monopoly law so that companies are able to go to court directly. It has also lifted the ban on holding companies, and revised the taxation structure to support this reform.

There have been a substantial number of new associated laws and regulations issued in Japan that had a strong effect on Japanese businesses and management. In some sectors these have not resulted in any drastic changes, and especially in domestic and stable sectors, the changes have not been that significant. On the contrary, there have been more changes in dynamic, technical, and international sectors, where the pressure for change has also been greater. Reforms made in the financial sector and telecommunications altered the environment of these industries radically to be more competitive. This left no other choice for Japanese companies but to adjust. (K.K.)

See also: *arubeito, freeter and haken, madogiwazoku, seishain sakoku*

鎖国

The closed country

sakoku, meaning "closed country," refers to the period of 250 years when the Tokugawa *shogun* enacted various laws that prevented foreign relations. To prohibit foreign influence from entering the country, foreigners and Japanese citizens were forbidden to enter or leave the country. If this law was breached, the consequences were severe, as the sentence was usually death. This policy remained in effect until Commodore Matthew Perry's arrival in Japan, which occurred in 1853.

Pioneered by Tokugawa Ieyasu, Japan was under the rule of the Tokugawa clan from 1603 to 1867. Ieyasu, the first *shogun*, was victorious in the Battle of Sekigahara, which enabled him to rule Japan. Tokugawa Iemitsu, the third *shogun*, inherited the title in the year 1623. When Iemitsu ruled Japan in 1633, he enacted various laws preventing overseas travel. In order to travel abroad, people had to become certified prior to embarking on travel to foreign soil. However, all of the certifications that were issued ended up being terminated and revoked after two years. Therefore, in effect it was illegal to leave Japan, and those people who violated this rule were sentenced to death. By implementing this policy, Japan became isolated for over 200 years. This is the longest period of peace reported for any nation in history.

This policy that the *shogun* enacted did not prevent trade from occurring; Japan still allowed private business transactions in Nagasaki with merchants from China. Holland was also allowed entry into Nagasaki, on the understanding that the Dutch did not attempt to promote Christianity. The business dealings conducted with the East India Company from Holland were strictly private trade. These transactions involved the *shogun*, but neither China nor Holland had diplomatic relations with Japan at this time. Therefore, they were only allowed to trade goods, which meant both parties separated economics from politics.

When Japan was isolated from foreign influence, the population and its domestic commerce increased rapidly. There were new emerging industries, which catered to new consumer groups. Also, agriculture was very prominent, and a main source of income for Japanese citizens during the Tokugawa period. Near the end of the seventeenth century, Japan became a highly civilized nation, with a developed education system. Increased wealth was accompanied by a more affluent lifestyle. As a result, people's taste for the arts increased drastically, as theatres and literature continued to flourish. During the isolation period, Japan was a civilized and peaceful nation because of Tokugawa's vast power and influence.

The isolation period finally came to an end when Commodore Matthew Calbraith Perry, a United States naval officer, negotiated with Japanese officials over many months to persuade them to open their country to free trade. America's agenda consisted of forcing Japan to open their ports, so the Americans could sail their vessels, disembark in the country, and trade. In order to accomplish these goals, Perry led four ships to disembark in Edo Bay. Upon his arrival, Perry refused to speak with people of a lower rank, insisting on discussing this subject only with higher-ranking officials. After nine months of long and agonizing discussions, Perry finally signed a treaty with Japan on 31 March, 1854. This treaty was a catalyst in opening up Japan to the rest of the world.

After opening their doors to global trade, Japan became a powerful economic force. When Commodore Perry forced Japan to open their ports, the nation experienced a sharp rise in numbers of foreigners entering the country. The rapid industrialization of the Meiji restoration, which followed the closed era, can be seen in hindsight as evidence for the relative success of the Tokugawa period under the *sakoku* decree. The speed and efficiency with which the Japanese synthesized Western lifestyles and values in the nineteenth century could be attributed partially to the relative stability generated by closing the country off to foreign encroachment under *sakoku.* (S.K.)

salaryman

サラリーマン

Company Man

salaryman, meaning a "salaried man," is often used in Japanese corporate contexts, and generally refers to a Japanese man who has a salary and works as a white-collar worker in a corporate environment. The term has been used for decades to describe the white-collar workers of the post-war generation, who have placed work above everything else. This in turn has led to the occasional use of the term with a negative connotation.

The term was coined by the Japanese from the English words "salary" and "man." It was first used during the Meiji Era (1868–1912) and became widespread during the decades that followed. The rise of *salarymen* was due to the strong economic growth that Japan experienced in both the pre- and post-war periods. The relationship between the company and the employee was characterized by mutual effort towards betterment. Since the bursting of the bubble economy at the end of 1980s and early 1990s, this traditional relationship began to change. While life-long employment, loyalty to the company, and hard work still played a major role, prolonged recession of the Japanese economy meant that companies began hiring increasing numbers of part-time workers, and encouraging early retirement of its senior workforce. This means that life-long employment is not now as common a practice as it was decades earlier, and is becoming increasingly difficult for individuals to secure due to companies becoming less interested in making long-term commitments to their workforce.

Salarymen are often portrayed as hard-working, yet lacking in creativity, initiative, and perhaps even a social life outside of work. This has much to do with the post-war generation, who have worked hard for their companies, which they regard as being a sort of family. These people sacrificed much of their free time by staying in the office working until late at night, and engaging in relationship-building activities, for example through golf and other leisure activities. This effort and devotion in turn led to a situation where *salarymen* had little time for their families, especially their children, which then led to the declining of the younger generation's interest in pursuing a corporate career. Thus, while the pre-war attitude of *salarymen* was positive, the post-war perception has changed to incorporate many negative connotations, such as long work hours, limited financial returns, a lack of prestige and status, and limited social interaction outside corporate relations. This is why some now try to adopt the term "businessman" instead of *salaryman*, in order to avoid the negative image sometimes associated with the term.

There are other threats to the traditional *salaryman* model, however. Rapid post-war economic growth fueled a seniority based payment system and guaranteed life-long employment, but after the Japanese economy's growth slowed down, more and more companies sought ways to cut costs. This is by no means leading to a steep decline of the traditional *salaryman*, but instead means that companies employ more part-time workers and gradually lower the number of their full-time *salarymen*, either by encouraging early retirement, sending them to subsidiaries, or by employing fewer new full-timers.

Despite the different attitudes and the changing environment bringing new challenges for corporations, *salarymen* have been and are currently still an integral part of Japanese society. This is evident from their long-term portrayal in various media, such as television programs, manga, and films. This in turn is continuously fueled by, and fuels, both positive and negative portrayals of *salarymen*. (A.L.)

See also: *giri, karoshi, kyūryō, marugakae, shūshin koyō, seishain, uchi–soto, zangyō*

seishain

正社員

Full-time employee

The term *seishain* denotes an employee in full-time, permanent employment. The term, however, has much broader connotations in a Japanese context, because this type of employment implies a much larger set of consequences and benefits for the employee, and may also refer to an official employee. In most cases, the majority of white-collar employees in large Japanese corporations are composed of *seishain*, making this group the backbone of the Japanese economy. About 20% of the whole Japanese labor force fit into this category.

Full-time employment does not actually relate directly to the number of hours worked or stipulated in the contract, but to the type of work contract; a part-time employee working full-time hours for an extended period of time will still not be considered a *seishain*. An employee is categorized as *seishain* when his contract specifies full-time employment of undetermined length, which implicitly means the benefits of life-time employment. The two types of work are also differentiated on the basis that the full-time worker is paid a salary, while the part-time worker is given an hourly wage.

An array of material benefits also comes with the status of *seishain*; the security of life-time employment alone is significant. Full-time status also allows the employee to receive all the social benefits provided by the companies, such as healthcare, or an extensive pension plan.

seishain are also the only group in a corporation to receive relatively frequent bonuses. In addition, full-time employment means that one can be part of the seniority based advancement system, and that he can expect promotions and salary increases over time.

Despite the extensive material advantages of the *seishain* over part-time workers, the true benefits of being recognized as full-time properly concern one's status. A *seishain* is acknowledged as an official employee of a company. This is of crucial importance in Japan, as being a member of the "group" (*uchi*, "being inside the group"), opens possibilities otherwise unavailable to "outsiders" (*soto*). The *seishain* often become part of the group as a new worker, as they are often recruited directly out of university. As an official member they can enter the *sōgōshoku*, the managerial track—where training will be provided, and they will have the possibility of making their way up the corporate ladder. This is a very typical career path for Japanese white-collar workers. The social status it provides is also of significant importance, as in Japanese society being a member of a large and potentially prestigious group defines to a great extent one's identity and the way one is perceived in a social context. Therefore, being a *seishain* in a major Japanese firm is extremely sought after, as these firms convey a great deal of prestige.

The fact that the Japanese firm provides for so much in a *seishain's* life comes at a certain price. A common feeling of loyalty and commitment towards their employer generally unites the full-time employee workforce. It is then customary to see employees working long hours of overtime or at week-ends without recompense, or taking a very small number of holidays throughout their career. It is important to note that the prestige and advantages of being a *seishain* are less and less attractive to new generations of Japanese, as this throwback often interferes with a new sense of liberty among Japanese youth. Paired with a high rate of retirement among an aging Japanese society, the number of *seishain* is in slow but constant decline.

A large gap exists between the number of women and men working as *seishain*. Women are normally less favored in this type of contract, as they are often thought unable to make a long-term commitment to the company, being expected to raise a family at some point. Indeed, a large number of women work full-time for some years before retiring, or take part-time jobs whilst having family obligations, although that is changing too with the younger generation. It is also much more difficult for a woman to gain advancement; as Japanese firms remain quite a masculine world. (J.L.)

See also: *arubeito, freeter, haken, shūshin koyō, uchi-soto, danjo koyō kikai kintō hō, salarymen, sōgōshoku*

sekuhara

セクハラ

Sexual harassment

sekuhara, abbreviated from the English phrase "sexual harassment," by definition is unwanted verbal or physical conduct of a sexual nature. This includes comments on someone else's looks, touching and groping, requests for sexual favors in exchange for rewards or in the face of the threat of being fired, etc. Harassment can be direct or indirect, with the victims being either females or males.

Japanese law distinguishes two types of sexual harassment. The first type of sexual harassment is that which uses a superior position or status to make sexual demands. The second type is sexual harassment occurring within the work environment, such as touching the bodies of female employees, or posting nude pictures. Thus *sekuhara* does not only include typical sexual harassment in its literal implication in the workplace, but also gender-related harassment, including of an institutional nature, stereotypical comments about men and women, failure to share information, excluding people from meetings, interrupting people when they talk, or sexual discrimination more generally. Thus, the concept of *sekuhara* comprises both sexual harassment and sexual discrimination, the latter being very subtle and hard to detect. A 2008 report shows that 8,140 women workers, or 64%, out of 12,782 plaintiffs brought sexual harassment claims, and 4,642 (or 36%) brought sexual discrimination claims. Another government reports from

2016 revealed that 30% of Japanese women in full- and part-time employment reported being sexually harassed at work. Among female full-time workers, this figure rose to 35%.

The term *sekuhara* was coined by the Japanese popular media and became widely used in 1989 with the Fukuoka sexual harassment case, involving a woman editor in a publishing company, and her boss. Three years prior to the use of the term *sekuhara* in 1986, Japan enacted the Equal Employment Opportunity Law (EEOL), to improve equality and rights for women. However, many companies got around the law by instituting a dual system of hiring, a complex system consisting of *sōgōshoku*, a career track mainly for men, and *ippanshoku*, an administrative track mainly for women to take up secretarial and clerical jobs, or simply to serve tea for their male counterparts. The EEOL was conceived to stimulate greater career aspirations for women, although it produced little impact on the working conditions and environment for women.

There are several discriminatory practices toward women that reveal labor market inequality in Japan: women's concentration in small firms, women as part-time workers, job segregation based on gender, the wage gap or wage differentials for men and women, and the glass ceiling, which suggests meager opportunities for promotions. Underlying these practices are the institutional factors that are deeply rooted in Japanese society. The tax system, which provides tax exemption if married women earn less than 1.5 million yen, encourage women to take low-paid jobs. Besides, the family is deprived of the provision of non-statutory fringe benefits to full-time workers if payment to the woman exceeds a certain amount. Also, certain laws and company policies for women's maternity leave, child-rearing, and childcare seem to be lacking or deficient.

From a cultural and societal point of view, the traditional belief of the ideal family formation—men working outside as *salarymen*, and women staying at home as housewives—still lingers, as many working women still quit their jobs after childbirth, and struggle even to get back to the same position, because of obsolete skills and their attention being distracted by family and children. Another factor that can be attributed to sexual discrimination is employment practice in Japan—lifetime employment together with the crucial role of on-the-job training. In the area of lifetime employment, personnel mobility is almost static. This explains why sexual harassment usually takes place by male seniors or bosses against female subordinates, empowered with the knowledge that their positions will not be threatened. Also, given the expectation that they will eventually be married and give up their jobs, women in the company usually gain the status of only irregular or contract workers, missing out on an equal chance of accessing training as compared to their full-time male counterparts.

This situation is improving as Japan gradually realizes how important the female workforce is, given that its population is both declining and aging. Moreover, younger and more career-minded working women are becoming more informed about the law regarding sexual harassment. Hopefully, in the future working women in Japan will speak out when their rights are violated and gain more support from society as well as from the legal system. (H.L.)

See also: *danjo koyō kikai kintō hō, shūshin koyō*

senpai - kōhai

先輩 — 後輩

senpai-kōhai system

The *senpai–kōhai* system is an integral part of Japanese societal structure and management, and is a seniority relationship system. The *senpai* is the senior person, whereas the *kōhai* is the junior. The *senpai* are usually older and have worked for longer in the company than the *kōhai*. As life-time employment is still common in Japanese firms, the *senpai–kōhai* system also applies to power and respect, as well as salary.

The *senpai–kōhai* system is present in many contexts, not only in companies. The Japanese apply it to the family, to school, to the company, and formerly also to civil law. This is mainly due to the Confucian influence from China in the sixth to ninth centuries. This makes human relationships the primary concern of Japanese. Respect for elders, filial piety, and loyalty, are promoted in Japan. The Japanese are deeply influenced by the cultural attributes of verticality, so *senpai* and *kōhai* use different *keigo* (polite/formal language) in communication. *sonkeigo* is used when a *kōhai* is talking to the *senpai* and honoring his superiors. *–sama* and *–sensei* are used when *kōhai* are referring to *senpai*, thus showing their respect.

The *senpai* in Japan acts like a mentor in the West; he gives guidance to the *kōhai* on both official and personal matters. This system not only provides on-the job-training and role models to new employees, but also helps the new employee adapt to the company more easily and to become more devoted to the firm. By supporting, teaching and sharing the experience of the *senpai* with the *kōhai*, a personal bond is established between them. Besides cementing this personal bond, *senpai* also help develop the connection between the *kōhai* and the company, by a process of socialization of the newcomers. The *senpai* acts as an intermediary, or cushion, between newcomers and the company. *senpai* help *kōhai* to adjust to the working environment and culture of the company, by teaching and explaining the operation of the company, and smoothing over any misunderstandings, in order to reduce any conflict between the newcomers and the company, and to enhance the unity of the firm. At the same time, besides the direct teaching from the *senpai*, *kōhai* should also learn by observing and modeling the *senpai*. Moreover, the *kōhai* is also expected to serve and obey the *senpai*.

Being a good *senpai* is part of one's responsibility to the company. A responsible, protective, and selfless *senpai* is the ideal. A few years later, the *kōhai* will become the *senpai*, and will then mentor newcomers. To prepare for this, employees discuss and note down the difficulties they faced in the first year. This drawing on their own experiences enables them to assist subsequent newcomers to become more easily adapted to the company. The *senpai–kōhai* system is like a relay which passes information, experience, and skills, from generation to generation in the company. Some *senpai* will become part-time consultants of the company to maintain the relationships of *senpai–kōhai* together with the company.

The *senpai–kōhai* relationship is not only a one-to-one relationship. For newcomers, all other workers are *senpai*, and others are responsible for teaching them the operation of different parts of the company. For women and part-time workers, it is difficult to find someone to be the closely tied *senpai*. Besides the officially assigned *senpai*, *kōhai* will also discover good *senpai* and ask for their advice. Furthermore, one *senpai* may not only be responsible for one *kōhai*. Such *senpai* and a few *kōhai* usually work as a group. The *senpai* acts as the group leader and the *kōhai* acts as an assistant. This creates a much closer relationship between them and shapes the leadership in the company. Former *kōhai* will also act as assistants to handle the new *kōhai* in the group. Different levels of management are thus created. (T.L.)

See also: *dōryō and dōkyūsei, keigo, nomikai*

senmongakkō
専門学校
Vocational school

senmon gakkō, directly translated, means specialization school, and it refers to vocational schools. Such schools, also called career or trade schools, provide occupational and professional education in which students are taught the skills and expertise needed for a particular job. Vocational education programs can be at both secondary and tertiary level. In preparing learners for careers in manual or practical activities, the term refers to traditionally non-academic subjects, rather than specific technical knowledge. Vocational education concentrates on theory and abstract conceptual knowledge, and it interacts with the apprenticeship system. Vocational education is recognized as experience of prior learning, and can account for partial academic credit towards a tertiary educational institution, for example at a university. In Japan, vocational schools are part of the higher education system. Students enrolled in vocational schools, study for a two-year period, most commonly after graduating from high school, although a high school diploma is not necessarily required.

The development of vocational schools has its origins following the period of the Industrial Revolution. Previously, the apprenticeship system and home schooling were the main sources of vocational education. Since then, the decline in various specialized handiwork tasks resulted in a demand for the development of vocational education. Efforts toward further advancements in vocational education during World War II stressed special training methods and practical work.

The history of vocational schools in Japan was initiated by the education system before the end of World War II. Elementary students were required to attend "youth schools," *seinen gakkō* (青年学校), upon graduation. These youth schools were a combination of vocational education, and basic military training or home economics, for boys and girls respectively. The aim of these institutions was to produce a class of professional individuals, rather than an intellectual elite class. In the pre-war period, higher education institutions for women were all vocational schools. In turn, normal schools that were often affiliated with universities, were renamed specialized schools, or the vocational schools referred to in the modern Japan education system. Vocational institutions throughout the country today provide a wide range of subject areas, including arts, business, engineering, fashion, law, medicine, and sciences, and cover numerous industries including information technology, retail, and tourism, as well as traditional crafts.

In addition to vocational schools for tertiary education, there are also vocational high schools in Japan. At the secondary schooling level, "vocational high schools," called *shokugyō kōkō* (職業高校), prepare students for immediate employment upon graduation from high school. While the mission of vocational high schools is to train students to start employment, academic high schools prepare students for the university entrance examination and for continuing education. The two distinct types of vocational high schools in Japan are the industrial high school (*kōgyō kōkō or* 工業高校), and the commercial high school (shogyō kōkō).

Modern vocational schools often collaborate with industries and work together to establish curricula for guidance programs. Cooperative training techniques for students, to engage in while they work part-time for a job they are preparing for, is also an emerging feature. Vocational education programs for employees involving apprenticeship and/or on-the-job training, as well as vocational education being offered at community colleges, are other emerging trends. The emphasis of vocational training has been maintained not only to improve the employees' technical instruction, but also their general work culture.

From the early vocational education programs, which focused on specific trades in the twentieth century, vocational schools have evolved and diversified significantly, existing today in the twenty-first century in numerous industries. They encompass a wide range of fields with the support of governmental and business organizations, due to the increasing demand for higher levels of skills and expertise from individuals in the competitive labor market. (P.L.)

See also: *sotsugyō, daigaku*

shacho (including all other ranks)
社長

Position Titles

In a common Japanese firm, positions are ranked from higher to lower importance as follows:

Japanese position	English translation
torishimariyaku or 取締役	Director of a company board
daihyo-torishimariyaku or 代表取締役	Representative director
kaicho or 会長	Chairman
shacho or 社長	President
fuku-shacho or 副社長	Vice president
senmu or 専務	Senior managing director
joumu or 常務	Managing director
bucho or 部長	Department head
kacho or 課長	Section chief
kakaricho or 係長	Sub-section chief

Although most Japanese companies follow the arrangement shown above, legally a Japanese firm only has two officially designated directors, the *torishimariyaku*, or board of directors, and the *daihyo-torishimariyaku*, or representative director, the latter being elected from the board of directors. Only the *daihyo-torishimariyaku* has the legal authority to represent the company outside its doors and to finalize deals previously approved by the rest of the board of directors. This position can be held by many high directors at the same time. In a Japanese company, usually either the *shacho* (president) or *kaicho* (chairman) act as the *daihyo-torishimariyaku*, and the *shacho* generally ranks higher. The *kaicho* is a former president who is semi-retired, who sometimes still exercises the power to represent the company, elect the *shacho*, and/or oversee the management of the firm. This practice varies from firm to firm, and his relationship with the *shacho* will depend on whether or not he has the authority to represent the firm.

In Japan, ranks are organized on the basis of the seniority system or *nenkō joretsu*. The lowest ranks within the company are usually given to the youngest members of the firm and the highest to the oldest. This is based on the supposition that the longer you have been with the firm, the more experienced you are. Since life-time employment, or *shūshin koyō*, is customary in Japan, this is usually a safe assumption, the oldest members having been with the company since they graduated from college. Thus, the *shacho*, or presidents, are rarely under the age of sixty, although lately some promotions have been based on attributes rather than seniority, making it easier for younger workers to become a *shacho*. In fact, top executives attain their rank mainly through internal promotions, which usually proceed in the following manner: from entry to the firm to placement in a non-managerial position; followed by promotion to a section head or *kacho*, subsequently followed by a promotion to department head or *bucho*; to finally become a managing director or *senmu*, and later a *shacho*, a top executive. Often an employee will hold the same rank in two different departments; for example, he might be the *bucho* both in the sales and research departments.

In contrast to Western practices, Japanese firms generally require the consensus of everybody within the company before taking any action. The decision does not just come from upper management, and is passed down the hierarchical ladder of authority. To gain everybody's consensus, Japanese firms use the *ringi* system, a decision-making procedure whereby members of different departments exchange information on their respective projects. This is closely related to the practice of *nemawashi*, where middle management acts as liaison in transmitting information to upper management. A typical example would be the *kacho* or section chief discussing a certain topic within his section, reporting it to the *bucho* or department head, who, after agreeing, would discuss the idea with his department. Afterwards, a *bucho*, a *kacho*, and a few *kakaricho* or sub-section chiefs from each department involved would attend a departmental meeting, under the direction of a *kacho*, where an informal decision would be reached and later communicated to the top executives. In this manner, lower management usually takes most of the initiatives in decisions and the upper management frequently just concurs passively. As a consequence of this system, Japanese directors usually lack individual leadership since the responsibility for their decision is shared with many other directors. (C.M.)

See also: *nemawashi, nenkō joretsu, ringi*-system, *shūshin koyō*

shain ryokō

社員旅行

Company trip

shain ryokō is the Japanese term for "company trip" or "company outing." Traditionally, it is a time when the entire company goes on a trip to bond with one another, build team spirit, exchange knowledge, and to relieve any tension in the workplace. This is also considered a "thank you" from a company to its employees, since most of the costs is covered by the company. Literally, *shain* is the word for "company employee" and *ryokō* means "trip."

In Western businesses, for the most part, the office environment is formal. It's possible to work relatively close to someone and know little about them. In Japanese companies building relationships with other employees is a vital part of working together. From an Eastern perspective, it is hard to work with someone if you do not know them. The *shain ryokō* is used to strengthen the bonds between employees.

When a Japanese company goes on a *shain ryokō*, all the employees lodge at the same place, enjoy themselves together, and build their relationships with one another. In a way, this is training for when they go back to work, so that they can more easily communicate with one another and function more efficiently than their rival companies' workers. However, for a large company, it may be too costly or too difficult to organize a trip for all of its employees—or perhaps it simply can't afford to close the office completely (even for a short time)—thus some may not do it. For these reasons, *shain ryokō* are much more common in smaller to mid-sized companies.

The trip itself is usually held once a year or once every few years (depending on the company and/or their current economic situation). From each person's salary, the company may take 3,000 to 5,000 yen and then cover the rest of the costs. Some companies pay for the entire trip altogether. The trip is usually a one-night, two-day outing even just to a nearby *onsen* (hot spring). However, depending on the company, the trips may become more extravagant. With more prestigious companies, the *shain ryokō* can be to places such as Guam, Hawaii, China, Korea, and of course the more exotic parts of Japan. Trips of this nature are usually longer than just one night. There is no set time for any particular company to go on a *shain ryokō*, however, in addition to going to an *onsen* the company usually does some sightseeing as well, and if the sightseeing is especially good at any particular time of the year (such as when the leaves change colors in the fall) there will be many company trips.

A related term is *gasshuku* ("lodging together," "training camp," or "boarding house"). In the martial arts world, *gasshuku* is when people of the same sports club go on a trip together and train harder than usual for a short period of time. Most commonly, this refers to students of a particular club going on a "training" trip of this sort. In Japan, club activities are quite possibly the most important aspect of college. Through clubs, students do most of their networking, and can meet former club members who are now in the working world. Usually these clubs are extremely strict and demand a lot from their members—so much so that club activities often surpass the amount of time students spend going to class, studying, and doing their homework. Due to the intense nature of these clubs, *gasshuku*s are not unusual. However, while the concept of *gasshuku* is very similar to *shain ryokō*, these terms are not interchangeable. *Gasshuku* is not used to refer to the sort of trip one would take in the working world. (R. M.)

See also: *dōryō/dōkyūsei*

shakaihoken

社会保険

Social security system

shakaihoken, the Japanese social security system, is classified into two main categories: social insurance and labor insurance. The former includes pensions, health insurance, and long-term care insurance; the latter, workman's accident compensation insurance and employment insurance. Full-time employees of a company are entitled to receive social security benefits such as health insurance, pension, employment insurance, and workman's accident compensation insurance. While full-time employees of the company receive a variety of social security benefits, part-time and temporary workers (*haken*) receive almost no benefits.

Japan has a universal healthcare system. Approximately 37 million full-time employees of large corporations, public servants, and their dependents belong to health insurance systems organized by companies. About 34 million salaried full-time employees and their dependants receive medical benefits through the Employee's Medical Insurance, or *kenkohoken* (健康保険), offered by the government. The National Health Insurance, or *kokuminkenkohoken* (国民健康保険), provides other residents, including the self-employed, with health insurance. Employees pay about 8.2% of their income to the government as an insurance premium. In return, the insurer pays 70% of the medical bill for each visit. Also, patients have a free choice of physicians.

All Japanese residents between 20 and 64 (including foreign nationals) also belong to at least one pension plan. There are two levels of pension system: The National Pension System and the Employee Pension System. The National Pension System assures basic necessities of life to all retirees, with a fixed amount of 66,008 yen per month, which is approximately 4.7 times the premium. However, full-time employees may receive an additional pension through the Employee Pension System, with an amount determined according to their age, the length of employment, and the contributions made.

Under workman's accident compensation insurance, full-time employees are compensated or reimbursed by their employers for work-related accidents causing injuries, illnesses, disabilities, and deaths. Employees are compensated for medical treatment expenses, wages during the leave of absence from work, maintenance costs, and disabilities and loss of employment skills caused by the accident.

Employment insurance provides full-time employees with financial support in case of unemployment and promotes reemployment. The insurance guarantees salary for between 90 and 360 days, depending on age, length of employment, and reason for unemployment. The unemployed are encouraged to reemploy themselves during the compensated period.

For the elderly, the Elderly National Health Insurance and Long-term Care Insurance systems provide additional financial supports. Under the Elderly National Healthcare Insurance, people aged over 75 pay 10% of medical bills, as opposed to 30% for other age groups. Under Long-term Care Insurance, patients pay 10% of long-term service expenses, such as nursing care expenses.

Japan currently faces social security problems related to increasing social security expenses, the decreasing number of premium payers, and changing employment patterns. Because the population is aging at a rate incomparable to other countries, medical and pension costs are rising drastically and the working population, who support these costs, is diminishing. Indeed, only 67% of the population contributed their pension premium in 2004, because they were unhappy with the system and doubted that they would receive pension payments in the future due to economic instability. Furthermore, the government is faced with the task of responding to the recent change in employment patterns, such as the increase of part-time, temporary, and female workers. (S.M.)

See also: *arubeito – freeter – haken, seishain, taishoku (taishokukin)*

kamiza / shimoza
上座 / 下座
Seating arrangement

kamiza and shimoza describe the seating order within a room. *Kamiza* refers to the "top seat" in a room, normally placed furthest from the door; *shimoza* is the opposite, the "bottom seat," often next to the door. On formal occasions the seating arrangements are of great importance. The correct seating position reflects the rank of a guest and is a sign of respect.

Rank and hierarchy are important issues in Japanese culture and are displayed through several modes and customs, such as language and gift-giving. Generally, older people are higher ranked than younger people, but family background, profession, personal achievement, and situational issues are also important.

In contrast to the West, where most relationships are seen as more or less equal, in Japan many relationships are perceived as asymmetrical, as for example the relationships between different generations in a family, different age groups in school or university, teacher and pupil, and so on. This asymmetry leads to the use of certain behavior or special language. If, for example, a higher-ranked person is talking to a lower-ranked person, the higher may talk casually, while the lower is supposed to use honorific language. This would even apply to a conversation between university students, if one student has entered the university one year earlier, and therefore becomes the *senpai* of the other student, the *kōhai*, who started his studies just one year later.

Normally the rank order in a relationship is defined when a relationship is established and conserved throughout this relationship. For example, if a *senpai* and a *kōhai* from university meet again several years later, generally speaking the *senpai* would still be considered as higher ranked. But there are several adjustments made to situational issues. For example, if there is a situation wherein one person is the host and the other person the guest, then the guest receives very respectful treatment, even if he would normally be considered lower ranked.

As mentioned earlier, there are different ways to convey respect to a higher-ranked person. The seating order is one important way to display deference to guests and higher-ranked people. The place of honor goes to the guest or the oldest or highest-ranked person, the lowest to the hosts and younger or lower-ranked people.

There are a number of rules for the seating order according to different environments. In general, the top seats are those which are considered as the most convenient and quiet. The top seat is therefore often the one furthest from the doorway and with the best view. The bottom seats are normally placed close to the door and may be associated with certain duties—for example, the seat next to the driver in a car would be considered a bottom seat, because it may include the task of giving directions; in an elevator, the place next to the buttons would be perceived as the bottom seat, since it includes the task of operating the elevator, while a seat at the back would be considered a top seat.

These general principles are adapted to different situations such as informal meetings, conferences or banquets, and to different environments. A Japanese-style room, for example, would have a different seating order than a Western one. This also applies to other situations such as restaurants, a car or a train, an elevator, office, and so on.

It is permissible to sit down by oneself, but it is still considered rude or unrefined to sit in a place that is above one's own rank. The host would have to ask this person, who had placed himself too high in rank, to move down to a lower seat. This situation is considered embarrassing for the host as well as for the guest, so it should be avoided if possible. It is, on the other hand, quite acceptable to humbly sit in a lower position. Normally a person who placed himself too low would be asked by the host to move up. (M.M.)

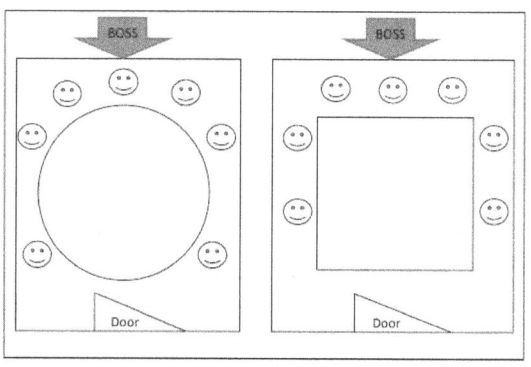

See also: *dōryō-dōkyûsei, gakubatsu, ningen kankei (jinmyaku), senpai (kōhai), tateshakai*

shinhatsubai / shinshōhin

新発売 / 新商品

New on Sale / new product

shinshōhin (products newly on sale) carry a sense of newness and fresh branding, which makes consumers feel they are ahead of the trends. The Japanese market is characterized by its short product life cycle. Company strategy is to dominate numerous market segments in terms of quality and design, to maintain the highest service levels, to differentiate their products and services from other companies, and to innovate frequently. Japanese companies do not respond passively to customers' desires, but drive changes that are advantageous when producing a *shinshōhin*.

As Japanese manufacturers produce new products they hawk them vigorously as *shinhatsubai*, or newly on sale. The business model is to introduce new items every few weeks, and hundreds of new products are born and hundreds die within a matter of months. Currently, after the burst of the bubble economy, Japanese manufacturers are scrambling to reduce the amount of new products and variations they introduce, focusing instead on pricing and repackaging. Nowadays, *shinhatsubai* not only concentrates on selling the new items, but also on effective presentation in the Japanese marketplace.

In the 1980s, Japanese companies started to fear the slackening of growth in sales of products as households in Japan already owned what was necessary for their daily lives. Thus, companies started to be creative in remodeling goods to motivate customers to purchase what is currently "in." In order to keep consumers interested in buying products, there has to be continual renewal. Companies have always created *shinshōhin*, because they have a constant need to release newer and more improved products over the previous ones. Additionally, new products are quickly imitated by competitors, so companies have to keep releasing new models and making improvements to keep pace in a rapidly developing market. (Y.N.)

See also: *shōkai, gentei*

shitauke

下請け

Supplier, Subcontractor

shitauke, "subcontracting," is an ambiguous term that has no true concise meaning, but is a term commonly used in Japanese management. Generally, *shitauke* is defined as a process in which larger corporations will hire small- and medium-sized firms to manufacture various parts and pieces of a project and assemble the assorted parts into a completed whole. Although the concept of subcontracting is widely used in several other countries, Japanese subcontracting focuses on the long-term relationship between large and small firms.

shitauke relationships are often beneficial to both supplier and contractor, as both sides assist each other in order to increase efficiency and cost. Certain conditions may be placed on the subcontracted firm, such as a *kanban* system, a process where subcontractors are alerted when an item needs to be replaced or supplied—but despite these conditions, the *shitauke* relationship is not exclusive. Just as suppliers are able to hire multiple firms, subcontractors are also allowed to have several clients.

Although not explicitly written down, a *shitauke* relationship is usually considered to be long-term connection between the two firms. As a result, both the supplier and subcontractor are able to make further investments in order to improve efficiency and cost. The supplier provides technological innovations to the subcontractor, as well as assisting with financial matters.

On the other hand, subcontractors are able to coordinate with suppliers more effectively in order to reduce costs and improve overall efficiency.

shitauke relations sharply contrast with Western subcontracting, where short-term relationships are emphasized and usually terminated after the contracted project is completed. Since these relations between supplier and subcontractor are unstable, investments that could improve the efficiency or cost of making specific parts are often considered riskier than in a *shitauke* relationship. Because of this increased risk, the benefits gained may prove to be marginal or non-existent, and therefore ignored.

In addition, Western subcontracting is becoming increasingly synonymous with outsourcing. As developing countries provide a new labor market where minimum-wage requirements are lower, Western firms are seeing outsourcing as a better alternative than subcontracting to domestic firms.

However, the *shitauke* relationship also makes it difficult to achieve industrial reorganization, as the smaller firms are usually locked into their role as a subcontractor. Despite receiving technological diffusion and reduced costs and improved efficiency, the processes are geared towards specialized products that only a specific firm requires. Therefore, several of the investments made by the subcontractor cannot be applied to other products, and thus are regarded as a wasted cause if the firm was to break its current *shitauke* relationship.

In addition, the burden of business fluctuations is placed squarely on the subcontractors, as suppliers can simply reduce their orders to reduce their loss. In contrast, subcontractors cannot easily find new clients in order to alleviate the reduced production, as their processes are specialized for a certain company, and other suppliers will have already established *shitauke* relationships with other firms.

Finally, similar to Western subcontracting, Japanese firms are increasingly finding the benefit of outsourcing to foreign subcontractors instead of following the traditional *shitauke* relationship. Due to a difference in labor laws, outsourcing to a foreign country provides greatly reduced costs to certain industries, and is often replacing *shitauke* as the preferred system. (S.N.)

See also: *kanban*

shōkai

紹介

Introduction

shōkai describes the action of introducing two people to each other. This can be done through a *shōkaisha*, a third person doing the introduction on behalf of both parties, or through direct personal introduction, *jikoshōkai* (自己紹介). This tradition is unique and important in Japanese business society because, at a first meeting, it provides people with instant knowledge about the status and rank of the people they are dealing with. *shōkai* often happens in business situations when introducing clients or fellow colleagues. Although *shōkai* can be used in the general sense of introducing people, business *shōkai* has specific mannerisms and expectations. The action of introduction will also take place differently depending on the people who are present at the time of introduction. It may be easiest to understand the introduction procedure by imagining that you are the *shōkaisha*, having to begin by introducing the lowest-rank person and leaving the highest-rank to be introduced last.

During self-introduction it is expected that you would state your company, your position in your company, your last name, and then your first name, in that order. When you are the *shōkaisha* introducing a person from your company to someone from a different company, you should mention their title first (with *no* personal connections—so one would not say, "he is MY managing director") followed by their full name. Conversely, when introducing a person outside your company to someone within your company, you should state the company name first and then their full name followed immediately by their title—for example, "She is from X company; Nakata, Yumiko; the Managing Director." Needless to say, a bow is required after your *shōkai* to show respect towards your new acquaintance and it is often followed by saying *yoroshiku onegaishimasu*, a formal way of letting the other person know that you consider yourself to be building a continuing relationship with him/her from now onwards.

When making introductions to a higher-rank person, introduce people from the lowest rank upwards. When a person from one's company and an employee of a different company is present, the person from one's own company must always be introduced first. When there are several people from your company, it is better to begin introducing from the lowest rank up to the highest rank, and where people are of the same rank it is best to introduce from the youngest to the oldest. Female colleagues should be introduced before male colleagues, unless they are older. If both are of the same position or rank and one is married, it is best to introduce the unmarried first. A family member must always be introduced to an unknown person first. (Y.N.)

See also: *kaisha, meishi*

shudanshugi

集団主義

Group orientation

Group orientation is the tendency to conform one's behavior, philosophy, or way of thinking to the group, rather than prioritizing the individual. A group oriented person would emphasize the benefit of the group rather than their individual ideas. In the collectivistic society of Japan, who you are is more important than what you can do. Being in a group provides a sense of identity and security, with, however, mutual obligation and a strong insider/outsider mentality. Due to Japan's history and culture, group orientation is prevalent in modern society and is practiced in Japanese corporations.

Group orientation is not a new practice in Japan. Japan is a homogenous island country which long rejected outsiders. By creating a sense of sameness and unity, Japan was able to keep foreign influence out of the country and develop a common enemy, uniting the dispersed country during the Tokugawa era.

There are two different types of group orientation; familistic group orientation and particularistic group orientation. Familistic group orientation organizes groups by biological principles, according to the idea that the family into which an individual is born is more important than what the individual is capable of. Belonging to a group is no mere theoretical relationship, but brings the sense of belonging, identity, and security. It is not just any group but one with biological relations.

This emotional fulfillment of acceptance is paid back by contributing to the welfare of the group.

Particularistic group orientation arises when the individual enters a particular organization such as a school, or corporation. When entering an organization, attributes such as age, gender, and school background are more important than qualifications. This inhibits merit-based salary in corporate organizations, but promotes instead the increase of wages by age. People in a specific organization will conform to the group they identify with. Being accepted in an organization physically, mentally, and emotionally is very important, and the fear of not being accepted by the group motivates people to work harder and to be acknowledged as a productive member of the group. Developing personal relationships with other members in the industry is crucial in a Japanese company, and is a way of creating social memory. Japanese society values tight-knit community and the respect for authority brought by networking. Because of social memory, people will cooperate with each other simply due to the fact that they belong in the same social circle. It is difficult for a newcomer to enter the inner circles of the Japanese industrial world. Entrance into this inner circle is gained through networking and affiliation from within the industry, and being in the inner circle ensures loyalty and cooperation. Social memory is important in order to stay in the social circle, since by being socially connected the individual will gain useful knowledge and information which will help the company develop.

Japanese group orientation emphasizes cooperation and harmony (*wa*). Harmony is obtained by the conformity of the group, which facilitates decision making. In group orientation, unity during the decision-making process is stressed, and the consent of the majority of the association is necessary. Since consensus of all the parties involved is necessary for making a decision, decision making in a Japanese corporation is time consuming. In a Japanese corporation, it is not the executive's job to give orders and lead the employees: rather, the executives facilitate the work by communicating with others and keeping everyone satisfied. They are supposed to listen to the group and accomplish the task in the manner preferred by the majority. (E.O.)

See also: *awase, honne - tatemae, wa, uchi - soto*

shūshin koyō

終身雇用

Life-time employment

The process of *shūshin koyō*—life-time employment—begins as a student. Students start job hunting (*shushoku katsudō*) approximately a year before graduation from university, and if they are successful, they will receive job confirmation (*naitei*) and be employed by the company that issued it as soon as they graduate.

Life-time employment relates closely to the Japanese *shudanshugi* or group-oriented mindset. The basic mentality for *shudanshugi* is the idea that every action and effort should be for the benefit of the group. With this mentality, Japanese who are employed under life-time employment start a life of dedicated service to one company only, and job transfers are neither socially acceptable nor even desirable.

Life-time employment has long been a benefit to both employers and employees at times when the Japanese economy has been experiencing success. For employers, it was a tool to increase the competency and skills of their employees, and the increased knowledge gained from this process would increase the worth and strength of the company. From the employee's point of view, life-time employment meant job security as well as in-depth training in their companies and industries.

Life-time employment involves all employees receiving extensive training during the early years of their career. Under life-time employment, a student's field of study is not important when employers consider applicants for job positions, because of the *jinzaikyoiku* (人材教育) or training that new employees will receive once hired. Newer employees are trained in the ways of the company (仕方 or *shikata*) and experience job rotation (配置転換 or *haichi tenkan*). This gives workers experience and knowledge of the company, which prepares them to be leaders as well as effective workers.

nenkō joretsu, or seniority-based pay, goes hand-in-hand with the life-time employment system. In a seniority-based pay system, workers receive salary increases according to time spent in the company and not necessarily according to performance. Those who have been in the company longer receive the higher salaries. Promotions are distributed in the same way. Therefore, managers and all upper positions are given to those who have been in the company longest.

In recent years, the lifetime employment system has faced challenges stemming from the rise in job transfers and the rise in numbers of *freeter* or part-timers. When workers transfer, the life-time employment system is interrupted, and the seniority-based wage system no longer satisfies or motivates transferring workers. Companies are becoming more reluctant to hire *seishain* or full-time employees for fear of the difficulty of laying them off during recessions. Part-timers are becoming more common because of their effectiveness and low wages. During economic crises life-time employment is hard to maintain, as shown by Japan's previous experience with the "bubble burst" in the 1990s.

Although it does have advantages, life-time employment is now on the wane.

See also: *shushoku katsudō, naitei, shudanshugi, shikata, hachi etnkan, nenkō joretsu, tenshoku, freeter, seishain*

shushoku katsudō

就職活動

Job hunting

shushoku katsudō, or job hunting, is a door through which many young Japanese are expected to pass; their lives will be transformed as a result. *shushoku katsudō* is expected of almost all Japanese, more as a fact of life than as a matter of decision. This places Japanese college students in a tight spot, since they are forced to make a decision at an early stage in their adult lives that may impact them for all their remaining years. The process of *shushoku katsudō* is difficult and long, but students engage in it since, even with the decline of lifetime employment, the core beliefs about lifetime employment still exist.

For many college students, *shushoku katsudō* is a stressful period, usually starting around fourteen months prior to graduation. The process of applying to a company is time-consuming, with each decision taking around three months to conclude. *shushoku katsudō* begins when potential applicants attend *setsumeikai* or 説明会, explanation meetings organized by companies for potential employees. Once they have decided which companies to apply to, applicants submit a resume. At this stage, some companies may ask for an essay. If one passes this, it is usually followed by a preliminary interview, a written exam, and up to four interviews, until one is notified—usually in person—about the decision. Applicants are rarely at ease during this process, since the lack of jobs is leading to ever-fiercer competition. The entire manner in which *shushoku katsudō* proceeds is one of intense psychological pressure. *shushoku katsudō* is not only an important step for the lives of Japanese college students, but it is also a step for them to be socially recognized as an adult, or a company employee.

A clear difference between Western countries and Japan concerns how people approach adulthood. In the West, it is the norm to spend a few years looking for what one would like to do with one's life. In Japan, *shushoku katsudō* is the norm for college students looking for a job. Job hunting is seen as difficult and urgent because many restrictions surround it. One of these is an age limit: the labor market in Japan is primarily open for fresh college graduates, and if one misses this chance, it will become increasingly difficult to find a meaningful job during their lives.

Lifetime employment and *shushoku katsudō* are two closely related ideas within Japan's hierarchical social structure. If one will be employed at one company until retirement age, then finding the right company is desperately important. On the other hand, with the restructuring of many Japanese companies, lifetime employment is gradually dwindling, and as it falls, so does the powerful impact of *shushoku katsudō*.

For many, the process of *shushoku katsudō* may be physically and psychologically demanding, but there are also positive benefits. One of these is a sense of unity. Japan has one of the densest populations in the world, and throughout history cooperation has been necessary for people to progress. In this sense, *shushoku katsudō* is something that the majority of adults go through prior to entering their "adult" stage of life. This contributes to a sense of unity among people as well as encouraging an even starting point to careers. (N.O.)

See also: *daigaku, ganbaru and gaman*

sōgō shōsha

総合商社

Trading Company

A *sōgō shōsha* is a special trading company which trades multiple kinds of goods. It is a commercial formation rarely seen outside of Japan. There are five major *sōgō shōsha* in Japan: Mitsubishi Corporation, Mitsui Corporation, Itochu, Sumitomo Corporation, and Marubeni. With the addition of Toyota Tsusho Corporation and Sojitz Corporation, they are called the seven big *sōgōshōsha*.

Three main businesses underpin the *sōgōshōsha*: trading, financing, and information. Trading and commerce include domestic trading, overseas import and export, and intermediate trading related to physical distribution. One *sōgōshōsha* may have businesses covering from 10,000 to 20,000 products—from foods and clothing, through automobiles, to steel. Financing is done by having traders themselves as customers. *sōgō shōsha* make investments by loaning to small industries and helping them buy and sell goods in a large global market, which establishes high trust and credit. In addition to low margins, *sōgō shōsha* aim to ensure the balance of supply and demand with long and deep *shinyo* made with their customers' industries. Data collection, analysis, and information distribution is done on a worldwide scale; one *sōgō shōsha* would normally have about 200 offices throughout the world.

sōgō shōsha own multiple businesses as affiliated companies. Ownership of each company, including the holding company, is characterized by cross-shareholding. In this way, *sōgō shōsha* create strong ties with each other and build a strong safety net through a balance of power and finance. The strong tie made by *sōgōshōsha* is a business system which has built up over many decades. The system has a strong corporate culture and tradition, originating in the pre-war period, and has had a great influence on the political system as well. In addition to high market share, the Japanese government accepts the *sōgō shōsha* as a highly efficient form of business that is deeply implicated in Japanese economic growth. Yet at the same time, the Ministry of International Trade and Industry regulates the *sōgō shōsha*—such a balance between acceptance and regulation is characteristically Japanese.

Today the new market conditions are presenting the *sōgō shōsha* with problems. Their concentration in low-technology industries is becoming a liability as the economy shifts ever more towards knowledge-intensive industries. In addition, automobile industries tend to have their own trading networks, which further limits the ways in which the *sōgō shōsha* can join the market. Other industries are following suit and avoiding using the *sōgō shōsha*; they prefer to establish their own trading systems to lower transportation costs and so lower the price of their products. As price competition is critical in the market, creating one's own transportation system is becoming more widespread. The need for *sōgō shōsha* is decreasing, and they now have concerns for their future. (G. O.)

See also: *zaibatsu, shinyō*

sōgōshoku - ippanshoku

総合職 - 一般職

Managerial track / administrative track

In many Japanese companies, full-time employees are separated into *sōgōshoku* and *ippanshoku* ("clerical") workers, hired separately. When recruited, future employees are divided into these two groups, defining their future work contents and career opportunities. *sōgōshoku* (literally, "managerial track") is a term for full-time employees who are engaged in core jobs that require "comprehensive" decision making, and who are expected to be future top executives in the firm. *ippanshoku* workers, as opposed to *sōgōshoku* workers, engage in general office jobs, usually concerned with routine subsidiary and administrative tasks like paperwork or possibly on a factory assembly line.

The terms *sōgōshoku* and *ippanshoku* came into use only after the establishment of *dajokōyō kikai kintōhō* (Equal Employment Opportunity Law), after which companies were no longer able to allocate all clerical and subsidiary jobs to women. Many Japanese companies used this system to circumvent the new Equal Employment Opportunity Law and place young female employees directly in the *ippanshoku* track.

Until recently it has been difficult for female employees to become *sōgōshoku*; women faced systematic disadvantages in attaining *sōgōshoku* positions, since they needed to consider marriage, working location, and children. In theory, a *sōgōshoku* worker will be promoted in accordance with abilities and performance but will also be liable to be transferred within the company. Depending on the company and the situation, *sōgōshoku* workers have a very high chance of sudden relocations, both domestic and overseas, or temporary transfers to subsidiary companies. On the other hand, *ippanshoku* workers have no hope of promotion but have the reassurance of knowing they will not be transferred, since they are usually hired by a specific branch office or factory unit. Wages are initially about the same, but *sōgōshoku* workers will get greater raises at a faster pace. At the same time, *ippanshoku* workers often receive fewer benefits.

After the year 2000, new types of *sōgōshoku* have emerged in response to the diversifying labor force and corporate struggles against the economic crisis. One example is the *chiiki gentei sōgōshoku* (limited work location system), which allows an employee to choose to stay in a restricted work location and so have the opportunity to build their careers without being transferred. Although introduced to give women wider options, this has also begun to attract male workers. Whether it becomes a permanent fixture in the Japanese corporate structure under current economic conditions remains to be seen. *sōgōshoku* employment for temporary employees is another example. Although *haken* (temporary) workers are employed for clerical jobs under normal conditions, it is not unusual for struggling companies in desperate need of labor to hire temporary workers for positions equivalent to *sōgōshoku*.

In terms of recruiting *sōgōshoku*, companies normally hire university and graduate school graduates on either the *jimu-kei* (white-collar) or *gijutsu-kei* (engineering) tracks. New graduates choose under which track to apply to a company, and usually do not cite specific occupations. Although not the only case, it is common that a typical liberal arts student with a humanities major will apply for the *jimu-kei*, and a typical student studying science and engineering will apply for *gijutsu-kei*. However, since *jimu-kei* has broader requirements (and from time to time will provide more job offers) as compared to that of *gijutsu-kei*, it is common for a science student to apply for *jimu-kei* but not as common for a liberal arts student to do the reverse. Depending on the company, the required educational backgrounds may differ. Some companies will hire high school graduates, and some will require graduates from junior college and up. Unlike graduate recruiting, mid-career recruiting for *sōgōshoku* will often offer for a specific occupation, since companies will hire candidates with a specialized profession.

The system has been strongly criticized in recent years and many companies have abolished it. The dramatic labor shortage that Japan has faced since the year 2015 does enable young women to also have career ambitions. The "classic" *ippanshoku* track is not offering enough career and salary opportunities anymore and it is becoming less popular (M.O.)

See also: *arubeito - freeter - haken, danjo kōyō kikai kintōhō, nenkō joretsu, shōshin koyō, shushoku katsudō, yokonarabi*

sotsugyō

卒業

Graduation

sotsugyō (graduation) is used only in connection with a regular course at school. Students who have graduated from school are called *sotsugyōsei* (卒業生 or graduates).

After World War II, the Japanese educational system was reformed and the 6-5-3-3 system (6 years of elementary school, 5 years of junior high school, 3 years of senior high school, and 3 years of university) was changed to a 6-3-3-4 system with reference to the American system. The compulsory education (義務教育 or *gimukyoiku*) period is 9 years: 6 in elementary school and 3 in junior high school.

Most courses in universities are built on credits, much like the US system. One has to gain a certain number of credits to graduate. The higher education system is divided into undergraduate study, bachelor's degree grade, 4 years; graduate school—master's, master's degree grade, 2 years, and graduate school—doctorate grade, PhD, 3-4 years.

The Japanese school year starts in April. It consists of three terms, separated by short holidays in winter and spring, and a month-long summer break. *shugyō-shiki* (a closing ceremony or 終業式) marks the end of the second semester in December, while in the third semester (January to March) in March, the *sotsugyō* ceremony congratulates students on graduating from school. In many schools and companies, the month of March means the end of the year. *sotsugyōshiki* are also held in

July and it is this ceremony that marks end of the first semester proper.

The program of a *sotsugyōshiki* consists of such things as an address by the principal, the awarding of diplomas, a farewell address by a representative of the current student body, a reply by a representative of the graduating class, speeches by guests of honor, and songs performed by the students. The most popular graduate songs are *hikaru no hikari* and *aogeba totoshi*. Before graduation all the students in the final, highest grade of the school take a graduate trip together for a few days, called *sotsugyō ryoko* (graduation trip).

Usually, universities and colleges (as opposed to high schools and junior high schools) hold big events for graduation. In the university graduating ceremony, female students often wear traditional clothes such as *hakama* or 袴 (a long pleated skirt worn over *kimono* or 着物) and male students wear suits or traditional formal wear. However, there are some universities were students wear European or US academic dress comprising hood, gown, and cap.

The school-based hiring system is the major way for high-school students to find a job after graduation. It is a matching system between senior students in high school and regular full-time jobs based on long-term relationships between high schools and firms.

In most vocationally oriented high schools, where most students enter the workplace directly on leaving, each school has control over a network of jobs with local employers and provides job openings and related information to its students. Under this institutional arrangement, called the job-referral system (JRS), many students obtain jobs through school channels and hence choose from the range of options their school provides. (P.P.)

See also: *senmon gakkō, daigaku, senpai – kōhai, ganbaru and gaman takokusekikigyō*

多国籍企業

Japanese Multinational Corporation

A company/corporation that generates over a quarter of its revenue from outside of its home country is considered a *takokuseki-kigyō* (multinational company). In the global market, being a multinational company is becoming the norm, but the Japanese *takokuseki-kigyō* are unique due to their values, standards, and mentality: lifetime employment, well-organized company training, seniority-based promotion, and long-term relationships being prioritized over profit. Thus, the Japanese *takokuseki-kigyō* is unique in that it heavily accents Japanese ideas and yet still performs well in the global economy.

The Western approach to business is traditionally "profit maximizing"; Japanese *takokuseki-kigyō*, however, value building long-term trust between business, provider, customer, and local community more than short-term profit. This makes long-term company management decisions easier for a *takokuseki-kigyō* because of its overall long-term vision.

Japanese firms are famous for providing lifetime employment (*shūshin koyō* or 終身雇用). This is a direct reflection of the trust-based society. The hesitation in firing an employee comes from the saying *girininjō* or 義理人情, which is the feeling of motivational moral obligation, duty, and humane feelings. The Japanese function under a belief in Group orientation, wherein group trust and a sense of obligation is what bonds people. Accordingly, *takokuseki-kigyō* treat the hiring process more seriously than in the US. For a typical college student, the process of job-hunting must start in their third year (junior year) and is expected to finish anywhere from six to ten months after the application is submitted.

Relating to lifetime employment, *takokuseki-kigyō* distinguish themselves by the company training they provide. Newly hired employees are expected to devote their energies to the firm until retirement, and the company invests heavily in them. The training is long, hard, and usually includes group work among the newly hired colleagues—the process of group work mirroring the philosophy of Group orientation. (Y.S.)

See also: *nenkō joretsu, shūshin koyō, shudan shugi (kojin shugi), keiretsu*

tanshin funin

单身赴任

Transfer because of job without family

tanshin funin can be loosely translated as "commuter family." Comprising two words—*tanshin*, meaning by oneself, and *funin*, meaning to set off for one's new post—this term refers to a situation wherein one parent, usually the father, has to move to another location for his job, while the family stays in the original place. The family is therefore geographically divided into two separate households. *tanshin funin* is most frequently observed in upper-middle- and upper-class families, and the member of the family who moves away is most often a middle-aged man.

tanshin funin is not a recent development in Japanese culture, but in fact dates back to Edo period (1601-1868). During this period, members of the samurai class were expected to relocate away from their place of residence if ordered to do so by their feudal lords.

While not unknown in other countries, this phenomenon occurs with higher frequency in Japan. There were 175.300 lone work assignments in 1986, but the number rose to 317.000 in 2004. Even though *tanshin funin*–type households are increasing annually in countries other than Japan, the number remains significantly higher in Japan; though while numbers are rising in the West, in Japan numbers have remained relatively stable over the last few decades. In Western countries, the employer/employee relationship is mostly of an economic nature, and there is little social stigma involved in changing one's job. The situation is very different in Japan, where a variety of factors contribute to a much closer bond between employer and employee. These include life-time employment and the age-based remuneration system (in which pay is based on one's age rather than performance), which serves to strongly connect the Japanese *salaryman* with a single company that he is likely to work for until his retirement. This makes it rather difficult for him to refuse personnel transfer to another location and look for a new employer, since under the Japanese system it is unlikely that he would be able to start at a new company under the same conditions. Four additional reasons contribute to the prevalence of *tanshin funin* in Japan: children's education, home ownership, care of elderly parents, and spousal employment.

Since most of the people who work as *tanshin funin* are middle-aged men, they often have teenage children in middle school or high school. Migration by the whole family would take the children out of their familiar environment, and could create problems for their education. This is especially important for *salarymen* with teenage children, as a stable environment is crucial for this age group. The second reason *tanshin funin* occurs has to do with home ownership. If the family owns a house in which they have invested a substantial amount of money, it would be economically unsound to sell the house, especially if it is unclear how long the duration of the personnel transfer might be. The third point is determined by the Japanese elderly care system. Traditionally, the parents of the husband live together with their son and his family, and if they do not then it is the responsibility of the wife to care for them. Since a migration to another city would cause many difficulties for elderly people, it is preferable to let them stay in the environment they are accustomed to. The fourth reason concerns the employment of the spouse. If the family depends on her income or if she is unable to change her job, it would be impossible for her to follow her husband to his new location. Japanese companies often support *tanshin funin* by paying for accommodation and travel expenses rather than encourage the migration of the whole family. (L.S.)

See also: *nenkō joretsu, shūshin koyō, taishoku, tenshoku, kaisha*

tateshakai

縦社会

Vertical Society

tateshakai is the hierarchy system that underlies all of Japanese culture and society, from the business office to the dinner table. It is one of the most important aspects of Japanese culture, defining how members of the society act and speak in every social situation. Without a thorough understanding of *tateshakai*, one would inadvertently offend Japanese people by not displaying the correct degree of respect.

tateshakai has its roots in the Edo Period, where a class system between samurai, farmers, artists, and merchants was created. It also has roots in the traditional Japanese family structure, where the father is the head of the family and younger siblings respect older siblings. Since then, *tateshakai* has evolved into a complex but mandatory system which determines one's place and dictates one's actions accordingly.

In Japanese society, status is determined by one's seniority and the prestige of the frame or group with which one is associated. Traditionally, the Japanese hierarchy has placed little emphasis on merit, using seniority and experience as the primary factor for determining status. This means that promotions to management positions and salary increases are often based more on seniority than individual worth.

Social interactions are dictated by *tateshakai*. For example, when two businessmen meet, they will exchange name cards and peruse them carefully, noting the other's name, and, more importantly, what company and title he holds. Each will immediately adjust his speech and behavior based on the other's status. The person with lower status will change his language to honorific, respectful, and humble speech, to show respect to the person with higher status. He will also be more reserved in conversation, doing more listening than talking, and speaking at a lower volume. The person with higher status may not use honorific language towards the person of lower status, and will express more of his thoughts and opinions. Another example of *tateshakai* influencing social interactions is seating arrangements. Within a group of people sitting at a table, the person of highest status takes the seat furthest from the door, while the person of lowest status takes the seat closest to the door, with guests usually being given the highest status. No two people can be equals under such a seating arrangement, which shows the extent to which the Japanese abide by *tateshakai*.

Showing respect to people of higher status is so important to the Japanese that one cannot even win an award for personal merit without feeling the need to complement the work of those of higher status. If a person were to receive an award for a book or painting, for example, he or she would humbly accept the award, while commenting that it is embarrassing to receive such an honor when older, higher-status people have not. In the business world, older and higher-status employees can make convincing arguments that they should receive raises and bonuses if younger, lower-status employees are earning more than they are. Furthermore, people of lower status will almost never openly contradict their superiors. In academia, one cannot criticize the published work of an older, higher-status person without first elaborately complementing the work, using honorific and humble language. In business management, *tateshakai* is the principle underlying many traditional Japanese management practices, including the *senpai–kōhai* system and lifetime employment.

The importance of seniority and its effect on a person's status is illustrated through practices such as the *senpai–kōhai* system. *senpai* are senior, older, and more experienced members, and *kōhai* are junior, younger, and less experienced. *kōhai* are very respectful to their *senpai*, who teach them and train them. Notably, the *senpai–kōhai* system is used from elementary schools to the largest business firms in Japan. Children are taught that their seniors must be respected, sometimes regardless of whether they deserve it or not, and that they in turn will be respected by their juniors. This lesson is reinforced again and again throughout a person's lifetime, so that status becomes essential to functioning, even in basic daily situations like sitting at the dinner table. (J.S.)

See also: *senpai-kōhai, keigo, shimoza, shūshin koyō, nenkō joretsu*

tenshoku

転職

Changing jobs

Although *tenshoku* can be translated as "changing jobs," the phrase in Japanese is much more loaded than the English equivalent. In stark comparison to the West, where changing jobs is seen as a necessity to further yourself in life, Japanese companies are traditionally founded on the values of a seniority-based system and life-time employment. These values, still extant in many large Japanese firms, actively discourage the movement of employees, turning *tenshoku* into quite the taboo subject.

In Japan, employment in a firm remains mostly based on the same pillars of seniority and long-term employment. However, over the past decade—since the bubble economy in Japan popped and the country was plunged into recession—many companies have begun to change their stances on long-term employment so they can let employees go in case of another macroeconomic shock. Many larger, well-established firms still offer long-term employment, however, since their size offers a certain degree of stability. In recent years Japan`s labor shortage has started a "War for Talent". Companies are changing their recruiting procedures and are more willing to hire mid-career employees.

Recent research compiled by the Japanese Ministry for Internal Affairs shows that the percentage of people changing jobs had been rising year up to the year 2008. In 2008 3.35 million Japanese employees changed their job, in 2009 3.19 million and in 2010 only 2.82 million Japanese found a new employment. The decreasing numbers were an effect of the economic crisis.

However, the number of job changers began to rise and peaked once again. In 2016 it rose back to over 3 million, 80,000 more than in 2015. This was the first time that more than 3 million employees in Japan had changed jobs since 2009.

The highest number of job changers can be found among the age group 25 to 34. 25 to 29-year-olds showed the highest willingness to change company (39.6%), followed by 30 to 34-year-olds (23.3%) with 40 years old and over at 14.0%. This shows that changing jobs is not seen as a viable option by the older generation. However, the number of job changes is expected to increase even more in the future years.

Many believe this is due to Japanese interaction with Western businesses, where there is much more freedom for movement. The fact that Japan is running out of workers is the strongest factor for employees changing jobs. The more competitive the job market gets; the higher salaries climb. Half of the respondents aged in their thirties believed that their salaries would go down or remain equal if they were to switch jobs, and only half of those interviewed felt it wouldn't be inconvenient to move.

From a traditional viewpoint, it is common to have only one job in your career: you start working at the bottom of the career ladder, progress up through the company ranks, and retire at the top. In this system, the companies do not need to invest much money into expensive training schemes, as all of the information required to be a competent worker can be learnt on-the-job over the course of one's career.

Given that there is a negligible amount of money invested in job training in Japan, workers will be wary to move companies as they would effectively have to re-start at the bottom, and may never overcome the social stigma of leaving another company. The actual social stigma attached to moving companies tends to be strong, and it is seen as more akin to disowning one's family than advancing one's career. In fact, Japanese employers are often suspicious of those who have changed their jobs, as those who do it are very much in the minority. Changing job is thus not a decision to be taken lightly. It is traditionally risky and unusual. Due to this, the market for middle managers in Japan is incredibly small, and nothing like as cut-throat as in the West, where workers are seen constantly jumping ship to stay one step ahead in the world of business.

If one takes into account all of these factors, it is clear why the idea of *tenshoku* does not fit well with the ideals that have been traditionally placed into Japanese minds due to the culture surrounding work. Therefore, the word is often used in more of a "career change" context, rather than "job change." If a Japanese person feels like they need a change of scene, and a totally different career, then that would usually be the only stigma-free way of leaving one job for another one.

The outlook of Japanese workers towards *tenshoku* is softening slightly due to the increased contact between Japanese firms and their Western counterparts. Many

Japanese workers now feel more empowered to make the switch between workplaces, especially if they have been seconded to work in the West, and now a large variety of Japanese internet job-seeking sites exist, where before there were none. The act of changing jobs has now become so common that a new word *jobbuhoppingu*, derived from the English "job hopping," has entered the lexicon. Although there are many connotations attached to *tenshoku*, the strong resolve against it appears to be weakening somewhat. (J.S.)

See also: *arubeito, freeter and haken, giri, nenkō joretsu, shūhin koyō, shinyō, takokuseki kigyō*

tsūkin

通勤

Commute

Commuting in Japan is synonymous with public transportation, specifically trains. The existence of *kuruma banare* (車離れ) or "demotorization" means that cars are not the preferred way of commuting in Japan. This is due to high maintenance costs and gas prices. In Japan, the car is seen more as a reflection of one's identity, taste, and income level, and in cities public transportation is a much more efficient way to get around.

The Japanese commute is a process of perfection. The trains come with intense frequency; at a rate of every 2-3 minutes. The combination of immense passenger volume and the numerous routes is undergirded by a strict schedule that is followed to the second. When a train is a few minutes late, the conductor will make an apologetic announcement on the speakers. Passengers will also receive "delay certificates": they will have to show these slips of paper to their representatives and in many cases their jobs will depend on them.

The most extensive and efficient rapid transit system in a single metropolitan area in the world can be found in Greater Tokyo. This is the largest metropolitan area in Japan, and consists of the prefectures of Chiba, Kanagawa, Saitama, and Tokyo. The subway system itself lies largely within the city center, but together with suburban railway lines it extends further than Tokyo itself. There are over 50 routes within the Tokyo Metro, and these carry millions of people daily. On working days, about 8 million people commute into the city, and with about 2 million commuters passing through it daily, Shinjuku station is the world's busiest transportation hub.

Japan has a sophisticated and well-structured train network, but only about 36% of Japanese train commuters are content with their way of commuting. Commuting in Japan means long hours. Trains are very crowded, especially during rush hour, and finding a seat is very difficult. However, with one of the best-organized and efficient public transportation networks in the world, Japan's train line is an example that the rest of the world admires and strives towards.

Japan Railways (JR) makes up of about 70% of Japan's railway network, with the other 30% belonging to private companies. Large companies such as construction firms or department stores may operate their own lines, forcing commuters to pass through their stores on their way to and from work and so generating significant business.

Commuting in Japan reflects the Japanese obsession with punctuality and efficiency. Train commuters depend on the trains' precision to be able to meet connecting trains. When a Japanese person boards a train they believe that they will arrive on time. One of the biggest criticisms directed at these perfectionistic expectations is that flexibility in society has been lost. Commuters in turn have lost their own sense of flexibility. They usually have a hard time when they go abroad and find that trains do not arrive on time.

The subway is essential in Japan. Neighborhoods are built around stations, and geographic locations are expressed in relation to the station that serves them. Train services cease at around 1 a.m. and start again at around 5. In a city that never sleeps this may seem illogical, but the heavy usage during the day means that maintenance is mandatory. In central Tokyo the nearest train station is scarcely a five-minute walk from any given point.

By international standards, the Japanese spend more time commuting than Europeans, North Americans, or other East Asians. About 53% of students and 48% of company workers use the train and subway to get to school or work; only about 24% of company workers use cars. 20% of the greenhouse gases emitted in Japan are produced by the transportation system. (S.A.)

See also: *yokonarabi, seishain*

wa

和

Harmony

wa is widely regarded as the most fundamental and all-pervading aspect of Japanese culture and identity. Although it can be translated into English as "harmony" or the "spirit of harmony," it embodies much more than these words suggests. *wa* was borne out of a fusion between Confucianism and Buddhism, which were adopted from the Chinese and assimilated into Japanese culture. Essentially, *wa* influences the approach that Japanese people still take to their daily lives, even though the concept is centuries old. It demands that people do their utmost to avoid conflict and cooperate as amicably as possible. *wa* is particularly prominent in the workplace, where it dictates the manner in which companies interact both internally and with other firms.

The Japanese character *wa* was derived from the Chinese *wō* and is the oldest recorded name for Japan. It was written using the Chinese character *wō* until the 8th century when the Japanese replaced it with the symbol 和, representing harmony or peace. This character is made up of the Japanese symbols for grain and mouth, representing a mouth being fed, and therefore the idea of a complete state of satisfaction and harmony.

The actual concept of *wa* is considered to have its roots in one of the seventeen articles contained in the "Constitution," as it was known, written by Prince Shotoku around 600AD. Rather than being a strict constitution, the documents were regarded as a set of guidelines to which government officials and their subjects should adhere. The first article, containing the definition of *wa*, provides that harmony should be valued, and quarrels avoided, and that when superiors are in harmony with each other and inferiors are friendly, the right outcome will prevail.

Despite this definition, the precise meaning of *wa* is very difficult to pinpoint. One way to view it is that everything a person does, thinks, or touches has a rightful place in the world, and their actions should not disturb the harmony of existence. Another interpretation is that those who strive to achieve *wa* endeavor to achieve a balance between individuals from different positions along the social scale who must cooperate in harmony and agreement.

Although the original notion of *wa* was spawned from a mix of Confucianism and Buddhism—and indeed the definition provided by Imperial Prince Shotoku has sometimes been viewed as Buddhist—*wa* is actually diffused and implemented in society through a form of moral, rather than religious, education. For example, students in Japanese schools regularly have lessons in "life guidance," which teach them how to achieve harmony in the school environment. These rules are promulgated by the Ministry of Education, not some religious sect.

In order to better understand *wa*, it is instructive to review its incarnation in the Japanese workplace and managerial practices. Business relations operate within the limits demarcated by *wa*, which emphasize the need for group harmony, mutual trust, and social cohesion. That is, at all times people must not take actions which may disrupt or adversely affect the group. In fact, group members in the workplace are expected to disregard their needs and feelings, instead focusing their energies on achieving group goals. This is consistent with the established tradition of lifetime employment; achieving *wa* is easier to do if one is sure that they will be employed for life. Similarly, managers will make business decisions which will have the most beneficial effects for long-term *wa*.

An interesting anecdote which helps to understand *wa* concerns the archetypal Japanese response to the question "What do you do?" Rather than declaring that they have a specific type of profession, the response, focusing on the group, will typically be that they work for a particular company.

wa is so pervasive that Japanese companies generally insist that business transactions and dealings take place between friends or companies with which they have an established and healthy relationship, rather than a company foreign to them. Establishment of close friendships is thus central to the concept of *wa*, as it requires that an agreement that benefits all members be reached on all matters at all times. This can result in false or apparent agreements being reached temporarily, so as not to cause commotion. This can actually be quite confusing for foreigners in dealing with Japanese, as it is not clear whether the Japanese are actually happy with the situation or whether they are just employing *tatemae* for the time being. Under the parameters consistent with *wa*, differences in opinion are usually resolved using a third party to judge or convey a message so as not to be too direct, or between the two parties in question at some form of entertainment such as *nomikai*. At such eating or drinking sessions, problems can be raised and discussed; however, in accordance with *wa*, they must be done subtly and in a way that is not offensive or harsh.

Even the traditionally harsh rules of contract law can be bent if *wa* so requires, as the Japanese view contracts as personal agreements that are flexible according to the situation. For example, a previously agreed price for an item or service may be subject to change if the supplier's costs change. One party is expected to agree to the increase in price if possible, to avoid violating *wa* and causing the other party to incur heavy losses. This is undertaken on the assumption that they will be rewarded in the future with preferential treatment. (M.T.)

See also: *honne/tatemae, nomikai*

wakon yōsai

和魂洋才

Western Talent with Japanese Spirit

A simple definition of *wakon yōsai* is "Western talent with Japanese spirit." This term is used to describe missions to the Western world undertaken by Japanese people in order to bring back knowledge about new things and use them to improve the Japanese quality of life. This was a task originally undertaken by the Japanese government in the early 19th century as a result of Commodore Perry's opening of the Japanese ports. The central idea behind this term was to acknowledge the superior technology of the Western world at the time but retain the Japanese spirit.

While this is a term that originated in the mid-19th century, when Japan was opened to the outside world, it continued as an ideology well into the 20th. After World War II, Japan was devastated, and the Americans opened the eyes of the Japanese people to consumer goods like refrigerators and radios. However, rather than just accept the usefulness of these technologies as they were, Japan chose continuous adaptation and improvement, similar to the Japanese business practice of *kaizen*, or continuous improvement.

wakon yōsai is also a term that can be applied to Japanese management. Its use in management became apparent with the creation of *zaibatsu*, which werelarge corporations based on the Western company design. The key idea behind *wakon yōsai* in management is that of taking an idea and molding it and incorporating it into the existing framework. For example, while the Japanese may have mirrored the corporate structure of the West by having large companies with CEOs and a vertical structure within the company, they retained their own society within the company through practices such as life-time employment and the seniority-based wage system.

This practice can still be seen in management today, as products on which the West previously had competitive advantage, such as consumer electronics or computer products, have shifted to the Japanese. This is partly due to their ability to adapt the products themselves, as well as a product of management techniques. Because of the way Japanese firms support each other within a *keiretsu* 系列 network, they have access to more financial capital, allowing them to take control of the market.

Japanese management has turned *wakon yōsai* into a success formula. The Western idea of publically traded stocks was molded into a Japanese concept by adding the idea of companies owning stock in each other, thus creating a stable and sustainable stock market characterized by shared risk. Within single companies, concepts such as life-time employment allow companies to focus on slow, steady, long-term growth, rather than just on the short term. (S.T.)

See also: *kaizen, nenkō joretsu, shūshin koyō*

yokonarabi

横並び

Going along with the crowd

yokonarabi is often referred as the "copy-cat" tendency of Japanese people, or their ability to follow the crowd (*yoko* meaning "beside," and *narabi* meaning to "rank with" or "line up"). *yokonarabi* behavior can be observed throughout Japanese history. During the Meiji Restoration, Japan sent government officials on a journey to Europe which enabled the Japanese to establish the Meiji Constitution and Japan's National Diet through adapting European influences. The Japanese aimed to modernize and become a world superpower through the adopting Western technology and its way of life. The Japanese understood that it was necessary to imitate Western powers in order to assert their presence on the world stage. The concept of *yokonarabi* can be observed in many aspects of the modern Japanese society, whether in purchasing the latest luxury handbag or buying the most popular new product. It is an important aspect of Japanese culture to mimic the behavior of others in order to be accepted in a particular group or frame. Although this phenomenon can be observed all over the world, it is more dominant in Japan.

yokonarabi also encompasses the ability of Japanese firms to closely mimic the strategic decisions of a rival. Japanese firms that follow the *yokonarabi* philosophy are often criticized for their lack of creativity in their products. The Japanese firm's attitude towards following or learning from the leaders of a particular market can lead to a lack of creativity in producing new products once the firm is on top. *yokonarabi* is deeply rooted in the Japanese business culture. On the plus side, it allows companies to monitor their competition and constantly make small improvements to products that are released daily into the market.

yokonarabi can be observed in the manner of decision making in Japanese firms. The heads of Japanese enterprises are more comfortable carrying out a plan that has already been put into practice or experimented with by a rival. If the plan is successful, Japanese firms will follow their rivals closely; and if it fails then the consequences are not so severe. In certain circumstances the heads of the research and development department of large enterprises may abandon their original plans and end up rehearsing the strategic moves made by rivals. For this reason, *yokonarabi* behavior is often deemed irrational. Japanese firms tend to exhibit similar behavioral patterns when a new product is released into the market. When a new product is introduced, many consumers purchase it simply because it is new, thus increasing consumer demand and interest. *yokonarabi* behavior allows Japanese companies to remain competitive in the market. This is the reason why Japan is considered to be one of the most difficult markets to penetrate, due to the intensity of rival firms. Imitating the actions of rivals has its advantages: it brings cheaper information costs, minimizes risks, and mollifies competition. In consequence, there are more *yokonarabi* products in Japan than in any other developed country. (K.U.)

See also: *kaisha, shudan shugi*

zangyō

残業

Overtime Work

zangyō means working beyond the working hours set by the company. The Labor Standards Act refers to it as overtime work, setting working hours basically as eight hours a day and forty hours a week. However, this differs according to the category of business and the job title. Where the workers work more than the legal hours, they would receive an overtime premium.

In order to be eligible to work overtime, the employer and the labor union must report as per the working regulations that they will be doing overtime work or working on days off. In addition, they must make an arrangement according to the 36 Agreement and report it to the Labor Standards Supervision Office. However, there are limitations to the hours of overtime work that can be undertaken.

There are three types of *zangyō*. The first one can be considered real *zangyō*: working for more than eight hours a day and forty hours a week and getting paid for the extra hours. The second type of *zangyō* is *sabisuzangyō* (サービス残業): working more than eight hours a day and forty hours a week while not getting paid any extra. This is illegal, so workers can charge the overtime premium to the company. However, if the worker does not charge within two years a statute of limitations comes into force. The third type is *minashizangyō* (みなし残業). This is legal if it follows the Labor Standards Act. This is a system in which overtime premiums for a set amount of time are already included in the salary.

The world's no.1 country for working long hours is Japan, where 28.1% of workers work more than 50 hours. Joint second are the US and Australia, with 20%. Next is the United Kingdom with 15.5%. There are many reasons why people do *zangyō*, some of which overlap—common reasons might be large amounts of work, not enough workers, and the overtime premium. *zangyō* has long been a tradition of business in Japan, where the person who works overtime is judged to be a hard and dedicated worker. Another traditional reason is because of peer pressure from boss and co-workers.

While *zangyō* provides for extra money and extra productivity, it has its bad points. The question has recently arisen as to whether *zangyō* is necessary; it is better, some say, to work efficiently rather than work for long hours. Moreover, costs for the company would be too high if everyone worked overtime. And death from fatigue or suicide due to stress—*karōshi* (過労死) and *karōjisatsu* (過労自殺)—is a huge issue.

Companies are trying to reduce *zangyō* to avoid the death and illness associated with its excesses. Firms strictly manage the working hours of their staff and an increasing number of companies are declaring No *zangyō* Days. Companies are also bringing in a system called work–life balance. Meanwhile, workers have responsibilities too, and need to find a way to work efficiently without doing overtime. (T.Y.)

See also: *karōshi*

3K (*kiken, kitanai, kitsui*)
危険、汚い、きつい
Dangerous Jobs,

3K is a contraction of the three words *kitanai*, *kiken*, and *kitsui*, and is a term used to refer to the low-class jobs that the majority of Japanese people would prefer were done by foreigners. *kitanai* means "dirty": in the context of the 3Ks, an example would be a sewer technician, a solid waste transfer station worker, or a sanitation worker. *kiken* means "dangerous": an example would be a highway maintenance worker or miner. *Kitsui* means "difficult" or "demeaning": recently, IT (information technology) work has been considered a *kitsui* job. Due to the tough working environment, long working hours, and lack of prestige, Japanese citizens have become averse to taking IT jobs.

In the early 90s, due to labor shortages, the Japanese government eased its immigration restrictions so as to provide special visas for foreigners with Japanese ancestry (known as *nikkeijin*; most were from South America). This was in order to combat the growing gap in the labor pool and divert the stream of illegal immigrants who took on work that was considered 3K. Often, those engaging in jobs considered 3K are paid considerably higher wages. (M.A.)

Contributors of This Book

Jennifer Brion	J.B
Frank Butz	F.B.
Alexander Chen	A.C.
Heejin Choi	H.C.
Todd Cisler	T.C.
Mike Estavao de Carvalho	M.E.
Michael Falkus	M.F.
Philippe Gagnon	P.G.
Josephine Gleason	J.G.
Jeremy Grant	J.R.G.
Christoper Grantz	C.G.
Kazuaki Harada	K.H.
Mario Harms	M.H.
Kazumi Hoshino	KA.H.
William Hundley	W.H
Ken Inagaki	K.I.
Hiromi Ishie	H.I.
Riho Katsuta	R.K.
Elizabeth Klaus	E.K.
Eric Krissmann	E.KR.
Katariina Kunnaton	K.K.
Susan Kwan	S.K.
Aki Laitinen	A.L.
Julien Levesque	J.L.
Haihu Li	H.L.
Ting Lin Yin	T.L.
Phoebe Lo	P.L.
Chrystel Marincich	C.M.
Ryan McClaskey	R. M.

Alan McMaster	A.M.
Shamyla Minegishi	S.M.
Taku Mizamae	T.M.
Michaela Müller	M.M.
Yuriya Nakamura	Y.M
Hiroshi Nakane	H.N.
Steve Nguyen	S. N.
Yumi Nishikawa	Y.N.
Erina Odaki	E.O.
Naoko Ohno	N.O.
Masaki Ota	M.O.
Grace Okada	G.O.
Charles Roum	C.R.
Yoshihiro Sasakawa	Y.S.
Lilian Schröder	L.S.
Jaren Shigeta	J.S.
Joseph Silcock	Jo.S.
Sukmawanto Arum	S.A.
Akio Takahashi	A.T.
Michael Teh	M.T.
Samuel Tuza	S.T.
Ken Uematsu	K.U.
Stanley Wang	S. W.
Maryam Allehbi	M.A.
Kathrin Kiesel	K.K.
Michael Kotzner	M.K.
Paulina Pirog	P.P.
Tamami Yamaguchi	T.Y.

Bibliography

Abegglen, J. C. (2006). *21st-century Japanese Management: New Systems, Lasting Values* Palgrave Macmillian.

Abegglen, J. and Stalk, G. (1985). *Kaisha; the Japanese corporation*, New York: Basic Books.

Akao, Y. (2004). *Hoshin Kanri - Policy Demployment for Successful TQM*. Productivity Press.

Alkhafaji, A. (1995). *Competitive Global Management: Principles and Strategy*. CRC Press.

Alston, J. P. (1989). *Wa, Guanxi, and Inhwa: Managerial Principles in Japan, China and Korea*. Business Horizons, Volume 32, Issue 2, March-April 1989, pp. 2–86.

Aoki, M. (1988). *Information, Incentives and bargaining in the Japanese Economy*. Ney York: Cambridge University Press.

Asaba, S. and M. Lieberman (1999). *Why Do Firms Behave Similarly? A Study on New Product Introduction in the Japanese Soft-drink Industry*. Columbia Academic Commons Reports. https://academiccommons.columbia.edu/doi/10.7916/D8TF04W8. Last accessed August 19, 2019.

Bailey, D. (2003). *Explaining Japan's Kudoka [hollowing out]: A Case of Government and Strategic Failure?* Asia Pacific Business Review. Volume 20, 1, pp. 1-20.

Bassani, C. D. (2007). *The Japanese Tanshin Funin*. Community, Work & Family, Volume 10, Issue 1, pp. 111-131.

bbc.co.uk (2001). *"Honne" and "Tatemae" in Japanese Society*, http://www.bbc.co.uk/dna/ptop/A571565. Last accessed August 11, 2019.

BBC News (1998). *The year the bubble burst*. http://news.bbc.co.uk/2/hi/special_report/1998/12/98/review_of_98/themes/232546.stm. (last accesses July 29, 2019).

BCCJ (2019). *Job Changing in Japan Highest in 7 years*. https://www.bccjapan.com/news/2017/02/job-changing-rate-japan-highest-7-years/. Last accessed August 1, 2019.

Benson, J. and Debroux, P. (2000). *Japanese trade unions at the crossroads: dilemmas and opportunities created by globalization.* Asia Pacific Business Review, 6:3-4, p. 114-132.

Beauchamps, E.R. (1998). *The Japanese Economy and Economic Issues since 1945 (Dimensions of Contemporary Japan)*. London: Routledge Dimensions of Contemporary Japan (Book 5).

Bird, A. (2002). *Encyclopedia of Japanese Business and Management*, New York: Routledge, pp. 344-347.

bijinesu manâ gaido (2019). *shoukai no shikata*. http://www.tisyk.com/cat0501/007/. Last accessed August 24, 2019.

Bright, I. M. (2005). *Can Japanese mentoring enhance understanding of Western Mentoring?*. Employee Relations, Vol. 27 No. 4, pp. 325-339.

Brinton, M. C. (1993). *Women and the Economic Miracle Gender and Work in Postwar Japan*. Monumenta Nipponica Volume 48, No. 4 (Winter 1993), pp. 513-515.

Broadbridge, S. (1974). *Economic and Social Trends in Tokugawa Japan. Asian Studies* 8, no. 3 (1974). pp. 347-372.

Black Tokyo (2008). *Number of Foreign Workers at Japanese Firms Leaps over Previous Figures.* http://www.blacktokyo.com/2008/09/14/number-of-foreign-workers-at-japanese-firms-leaps-over-previous-figures/. Last accessed August 19, 2019.

BusinessDictionary.com - Online Business Dictionary (2019). *Contract*. http://www.businessdictionary.com/definition/contract.html. Last accessed August 1, 2019.

Cabuloy, M. and Aoki, M. (2009). *Distribution*. In: P. Haghirian (Ed.). J-Management Fresh Perspectives on the Japanese Firm in the 21st Century. i-universe Press.

Carlet, L. (2004). *Workplace Worries*. The Japan Times, December 21, 2004. http://search.japantimes.co.jp/cgi-bin/fl20041221zg.html. Last accessed December 12, 2009.

Chen, M. (1995). *Asian Management Systems - Chinese, Japanese and Korean Style of Business*. Thomson Learning.

Citizendium (2019). *Japanese Language*. http://en.citizendium.org/wiki/Japanese_language. Last accessed August 1, 2019.

Colignon, R. and Usui, C. (2003). *Amakudari. The Hidden Fabric of Japan's Economy*. Ithaca, NY: Cornell University Press.

Community for Human Resource Management (2019). *The Lean Thinking: Mura, Muri, Muda*. http://www.chrmglobal.com/Articles/485/1/The-Lean-Thinking--Mura-Muri-Muda.html. Last accessed August 1, 2019.

Crocker, O., Chiu, J.S.L. and Charney, C. (1984). *Quality Circles*, Toronto: Methuen.

Davies, R. J. and Ikeno, O. (2002). *The Japanese Mind: Understanding Comtemporary Japanese Culture*. (1st ed.). Tokyo: Tuttle Publishing.

De Mente, B. (2004). *Japan's Cultural Code Words*. Tokyo: Tuttle Publishing.

De Mente, B. (2004). *Japanese Etiquette & Ethics in Business* (6th ed.). Boston: McGraw-Hill.

Department of the Navy (2019). *Brief Summary of the Perry Expedition to Japan, 1853*. https://www.history.navy.mil/content/history/nhhc/research/library/online-reading-room/title-list-alphabetically/b/brief-summary-perry-expedition-japan-1853.html. Last accessed August 23, 2019.

Doi, T. (1973). *The Anatomy of Dependence*. New York: Kodansha International.

Donahue, R.T. (1998). *Japanese Culture and Communication—Critical Cultural Analysis*. University Press of America.

Douglass, M. and Roberts, G. (2015). *Japan and Global Migration – Foreign workers and the advent of a multicultural society*. London: Routledge (Reprint).

Dziesinski, M. (2008). *From Failed Sons to Working Mean: Rehabilitating Hikikomori*. American Sociological Association Paper. http://socialsciences.people.hawaii.edu/publications_lib/DZIESINSKI_ASA_From_Failed_Sons.pdf. Last accessed August 1, 2019.

Encyclopedia.com (2019). old-boy network. *The Oxford Pocket Dictionary of Current English*. 2009. Online Version. https://www.encyclopedia.com/humanities/dictionaries-thesauruses-pictures-and-press-releases/old-boy-network. Accessed August 11, 2019.

Encyclopedia of Japanese Culture (2019). *Nengajo to Shochumimai*. http://iroha-japan.net/iroha/B06_custom/06_nengajo.html. Last accessed August 1, 2019.

Factories Strategy Groups (2009). *Hansei Resources*. http://www.superfactory.com/topics/hansei.html. Last accessed December 12, 2009.

Fleckenstein, B. (2005). *Contrarian Chronicles-Lessons from Japan's bubble - for ours*.

http://www.wallstreetbear.com/board/view.php?topic=30885&post=101197c, cited July 10, 2012.

Fukukawa, S. (1999). *Japan's Challenge for Economic Revitalization*. Dentsu Institute for Human Studies. https://academiccommons.columbia.edu/doi/10.7916/D8FN1DS8. Last accessed August 24, 2019.

Fusanosuke, N. (2003). *Japanese Manga: Its Expression and Popularity*. ABD 2003, Volume 34, Number 1. https://www.accu.or.jp/appreb/09/pdf34-1/34-1P003-005.pdf. Last accessed August 19, 2019.

Gakken (1999). *Pictorial Encyclopedia of Japanese Life and Events*. Tokyo: Gakken, pp. 98-110.

Genda, Y., Kondo, A. and S. Ohta (2007). *Long-term effects of a recession at labor market entry in Japan and The United States*. http://www.e.u-tokyo.ac.jp/cirje/research/workshops/macro/documents/macro0607.pdf. Last accessed December 12, 2009.

Genzberger, C. and E. G. Hinkelman (1994). *Japan Business: The Portable Encyclopedia for Doing Business with Japan*. World Trade Press.

Gravett, P. (2004). *Manga: 60 Years of Japanese Comics*. Harper Design.

Guardian, The. (2009). *Japan looks to manga comics to rescue ailing economy*. https://www.theguardian.com/world/2009/apr/10/japan-manga-anime-recession. Last accessed August 1, 2019.

Hadamitzky, W. and Spahn, M. (1981). *Kanji and Kana*. Boston: Tuttle.

Haghirian, P. (2009): *J-Management*. iUniverse Press.

Hanazaki, M. (2001). *An International Comparison of Corporate Investment Behavior-Some Implications for the Governance Structure in Japan*. Center for Economic Institutions Working Paper Series, February 2001. hermes-ir.lib.hit-u.ac.jp/rs/bitstream/10086/13971/1/wp2001-1a.pdf. Last accessed August 19, 2019.

Hart, R. and S. Kawasaki (1999). *Work and Pay in Japan*. Cambridge: Cambridge University Press.

Hatena Keyword (2019). *zangyo*. http://d.hatena.ne.jp/keyword/%BB%C4%B6%C8. Last accessed August 19, 2019.

Hemmi, C. (2006). *'Ganbarism', an art in the craft of collaborative learning*. Available: http://associates.iatefl.org/pages/materials/voicespdf/cp5.pdf. Last accessed 12 December 2009.

Henshall, K. G. (1999). *Dimensions of Japanese Society: Gender, Margins and Mainstream*. New York: Palgrave Macmillan.

Higuchi, Y. (2005). *Baby-boom Generation Approaches Retirement Age: Coping with a Depopulating Society*. Japanese Institute of Global Communications. http://www.glocom.org/debates/20050421_nomura_comment/. Last accessed August 11, 2019.

Hirschmeier, J. and Yui, T (1975). *The Development of Japanese Business 1600-1973*. Cambridge, USA: Harvard University Press.

Hodgson, J. (2007). *Doing Business with the New Japan: Succeeding in America's Richest International*. Rowman & Littlefield Publishers, Inc. Second edition.

Horioka, Y. (2004). *Are the Japanese unique? An Analysis of Consumption and Saving Behavior in Japan*. ISER Discussion Paper No. 606. https://papers.ssrn.com/sol3/papers.cfm?abstract_id=558003. Last accessed August 1, 2019.

Hrannac, M. and Brannen, M. (1982). *The What, Where, and Whys of Quality Control Circle*. In: *Management by Japanese Systems*. Lee, S. M. and G. Schwendiman (Eds.). New York: Praeger Publishers.

Hurry, D. (1993). *Restructuring in the Global Economy: The Consequences of Strategic Linkages Between Japanese and U.S. Firms*. Strategic Management Journal, Volume 14, Special Issue: Corporate Restructuring, pp. 69-82.

Hutchins, D. (2008). *Hoshin Kanri - The Strategic Approach to Continuos Improvement*. New York: Routledge.

Imai, M. (1986). *Kaizen –the Key to Japan's Competitive Success*. New York: Random House Business.

Imai M. (2007). *Gemba Kaizen: A Commonsense Low-cost Approach to Management*. New York: McGraw-Hill Professional, p. 13.

Inohara, H. (1997). *Human Resource Development in Japanese Companies*. Tokyo: Asian Productivity Organization.

Isa, K. and Tsuru T. (2002). *Cell Production and Workplace Innovation in Japan: Toward a New Model for Japanese Manufacturing?* Industrial Relations, Volume 41, pp. 548 - 578.

Jacob, G. W. (1982). *Quality Circles and Japanese Management: Participation or Paternalism?*. In: Sang M. Lee and Gary Schwendiman (Eds.). Management by Japanese Systems. New York: Praeger Publishers.

Japan Federation of Bar Associations (2019). *The Japanese Attorney System*. http://www.nichibenren.or.jp/en/about/judicial_system/attorney_system.html. Accessed August 11, 2019.

Japan-Guide.com (2019). *Takuhaibin Delivery Services*. http://www.japan-guide.com/e/e2278.html. Last accessed August 11, 2019.

Jeong, D. Y. and Aguilera, R. (2008). *The Evolution of Enterprise Unionism in Japan: A Socio-Political Perspective*. British Journal of Industrial Relations, Volume 46/1, p. 98 – 132.

JOPUS (2019). *Younger professionals in Japan changing jobs more often, at an average age of 32*. https://jopus.net/en/news/doda-average-age.html. Last accessed February 8, 2019.

Kageyama, Y. (2009). *Cars no longer coveted by young*. Japan Times, January 4, 2009. https://www.japantimes.co.jp/news/2009/01/04/national/cars-no-longer-coveted-by-young/#.XV9J4XsRU2w. Last accessed August 23, 2019.

Katahira, H, Mizuno, M. and Yoram Wind (1993). *New Product Success in the Japanese Consumer Goods Market*. SEI Center for Advanced Studies in Management, The Wharton School, Working Paper, 1993.

Kato, H. and Kato, J. S. (1992). *Understanding and Working with the Japanese Business World* Prentice Hall.

Katz, R. (1998). *Japan: The System that Soured*. New York: M.E. Sharp.

Katz, R. (2001). *Chapter 3 Update: Hollowing Out Accelerates in the Late 1990's*. Japanese Economy. September – December 2001. Volume 29, Issue 5/6. p. 20-28.

Kazui, T. (1982). *Foreign Relations during the Edo Period: Sakoku Reexamined. Translated by Susan Videen*. Journal of Japanese Studies Volume 8, No. 2 (1982): pp. 283-306.

Keeley, T. D. (2001). *International Human Resource Management in Japanese Firms: Their Greatest Challenge*. New York: Palgrave MacMillan.

Khan, S. and H. Yoshihara (1994). *Strategy and Performance of Foreign Companies in Japan*. Praeger.

Khojasteh, Y. (2016): *Kaizen*. In: Haghirian, P. (Ed.) The Routledge Handbook of Japanese Business and Management. Abingdon-on-Thames: Routledge.

Kijima, N. (2001). *Bento Boxes: Japanese Meals on the Go*. Tokyo: Japan Publications Trading.

Kimura, F. (2002). *Subcontracting and the Performance of Small and Medium Firms in Japan*. Small Business Economics, February 2002, Volume 18, Issue 1–3, pp 163–175.

Kimura, O. and Terada, H. (1981). *Design and Analysis of Pull System, A Method of Multi-Stage Production Control*. International Journal of Production Research, No. 19,3: p. 241 - 53.

Koh, M. (2003). *Kenkyusha's New Japanese-English Dictionary, 4th ed.* Tokyo: Kenkyusha.

Koike, K. (1988). *Understanding Industrial Relations in Modern Japan*. Palgrave Macmilan.

Koizumi, K. (2002). *In Search of "Wakon": The Cultural Dynamics of the Rise of Manufacturing Technology in Postwar Japan*. Technology and Culture Volume 43, Issue 1 (2002): pp. 29-49.

Kopp, R. (2000). *The Rice-Paper Ceiling: Breaking Through Japanese Corporate Culture*. Stone bridge press.

Kosugi, R. (2006). *Youth Employment in Japan's Economic Recovery: 'Freeters' and 'NEETs'*. Japan Focus, 11 May 2006. http://www.japanfocus.org/-Kosugi_Reiko/2022. Last accessed August 1, 2019.

Kotler, P., Keller, K., Ang, S., Leong, S. and Tan, C. (2006). *Marketing Management: an Asian Perspective*. Pearson Education Centre.

Koyama-Richard, B. (2014). *One thousand years of manga*. Flammarion.

Kristoff, N. D. (1997). *Where Children Rule*. New York Times, August 17, 1997. http://www.nytimes.com/1997/08/17/magazine/where-children-rule.html?scp=3&sq=hansei&st=cse, *New York Times* (last accessed August 1, 2019).

Kwintessential.co.uk (2019). *A Guide to Japan – Etiquette, Customs, Clothing and More*. https://www.kwintessential.co.uk/resources/guide-to-japan-etiquette-customs-culture-business. Last accessed August 1, 2019.

Kyodo (2018a). *Sales of digital Manage overtake print editions in Japan for the first time*. Japan Times, February 26, 2018. https://www.japantimes.co.jp/news/2018/02/26/national/sales-digital-manga-overtake-print-editions-japan-first-time/#.XVzztHsRU2w. Last accessed August 1, 2019.

Kyodo (2018b). *Japan sets goals for companies to prevent deaths from overwork*. https://www.japantimes.co.jp/news/2018/05/31/national/japan-sets-goals-companies-prevent-deaths-overwork/#.XNPsxU17mP8. Accessed March 30, 2019.

Lam, A. C.L. (1992). *Women and Japanese Management, Discrimination and Reform*. New York: Routledge.

Langley Esquire (2012). *Lawyers in Japan*. http://www.langleyesquire.com/about/lawyers-in-japan. accessed March 5, 2012).

Liker, J. (2004). *The Toyota Way*. McGraw-Hill.

Matthews, G. and White, B. (2004). *Japan's Changing Generations; Are Young People Creating a New Society?* Routledge, Japan Anthropology Workshop Series.

McCreery, J. (2000). *Japanese Consumer Behavior: from Worker Bees to Wary Shoppers*. London: Routledge.

McCurry, J. (2016). Nearly a third of Japan's women 'sexually harassed at work'. The Guardian, March 2, 2016. https://www.theguardian.com/world/2016/mar/02/japan-women-

sexually-harassed-at-work-report-finds. Last accessed September 11, 2019.
McDaniel, E, R. and E. Katsumata (2006): *Enculturation of values in the Educational Setting: Japanese group Orientation*. Intercultural communication: a reader: Boston, USA: Wadsworth Cengage Learning: pp. 365-376.
McGwire, J. and Dow, S. (2009). *Japanese Keiretsu: Past, Present and Future*. Asia Pacific Journal of Management, Volume 26, Issue 2, p. 333 - 351.
McClain, J. (2002). *Japan: A Modern History*. W. W. Norton & Company
Mehri, D. (2005). *Notes from Toyota-land: An American Engineer in Japan*, Cornell University Press, New York.
Mino, H. (2009). *A Study on the Japanese People's Social Behavior: Part One From a Historical Point of View: Yokonarabi Behavior and The Countervailing Force to the Social Trend*. https://www.scribd.com/document/79184777/Japanes-Behavior-Study. Last accessed August 19, 2019.
Morishima, M. (2007). *Seikashugi from an Employee Perspective*. Research Gate: https://www.researchgate.net/publication/237742698_Seikashugi_from_an_Employee_Perspective. Last accessed August 19, 2019.
Motoe, T. (2006). *anata no kaisha wa daijôbu? sâbisu zangyo. Is your company all right? Service Zangyo. All About*. http://allabout.co.jp/family/lawabc/closeup/CU20060119B/. Last accessed August 19, 2019.
Mukuno, M. and K. Tanaka *(2018). hajimete no shakaihosho*. Tokyo: Yuhikaku Publishing.
Nagase, K. (2002). *Contracts*. In: Bird, A. (2002). *Encyclopedia of Japanese Business and Management*, New York: Routledge.
Nagata, K. (2009). *The Uphill Battle Against 'DescentfFrom Heaven*. The Japan Times. February 10, 2009.
Nagesh, R. and N. Yoshino. (2008). *An Empirical Analysis of Japanese Banking Behavior in a Period of Financial Instability*. Keio Economic Studies, Volume 45, Issue 1.
Nakagawa, R. (2008). *Herd Behavior by Japanese Banks in Local Financial Markets*. Working Paper at the Faculty of Economics, Kansai University https://pdfs.semanticscholar.org/a374/97efd1952e03b07e86b3e7875f2463f8f3b1.pdf. Last accessed August 24, 2019.
Nakamura A. (2004). *Being NEET not so neat for nation's youth*. The Japan Times, 19 June 2004. http://search.japantimes.co.jp/print/news/nn06-2004/nn20040619f2.htm. Last accessed November 16, 2009.
Nakane, C. (1983). *Tateshakai no ningen kankei*. Tokyo: Kodansha.
Nakane, C. (1991). *Japanese Society*, Tokyo: Tuttle Co. Publishers.
Nakata, H. (2008). *Low key, off key, but anyway it's your way*. The Japan Times Online. 1 July 2008. http://search.japantimes.co.jp/cgi-bin/nn20080701i1.html
Nakayama, Y. (2019). *The Violence of Shushoku Katsudo*. http://themargins.net/fps/student/nakayama.html. Last accessed August 23, 2019.
Naoi, A. and Schooler, C. (1985). *Occupational Conditions and Psychological Functioning in Japan*. The American Journal of Sociology, Volume 90, No. 4, January 1985, pp. 729-752.
nbakki (2019). *Number of Lawyers in Japan by Prefecture, 2018*. http://nbakki.hatenablog.com/entry/Number_of_Lawyers_in_Japan_by_Prefecture_2018. Last accessed September 11, 2019.

Nengajou Hakubutsukan (2019). *Nengajo no rekishi*. http://www.nengahaku.jp/history-3.html. Last accessed August 2, 2019.

Nishida, J. and Sanga A. (2009). *Marketing*. In: P. Haghirian (Ed.). J-Management Fresh Perspectives on the Japanese Firm in the 21st Century. i-universe Press.

Nishiguchi, K. (2009). トヨタ生産方. http://www-h.yamagata-u.ac.jp/~yin/seminar2004/TPS.pdf. Last accessed December 16, 2009.

Nishiyama, K. (2000). *Doing Business with Japan: Successful Strategies for Intercultural Communication*. Latitude 20 Books.

Nishiyama, K. and Johnson, J. (2007). *Work Health, Karoshi-Death from Overwork: Occupational Health Consequences of the Japanese Production Management*. www.workhealth.com. Last accessed August 1, 2019.

NRI (Nomura Research Institute) (2004). *Over 90% of People Have a Sense of Crisis Regarding the NEET Issue*. http://www.nri.co.jp/english/news/2004/041101.html. Last accessed December 12, 2009.

Ogura, S., Tachibanaki, T. and Wise, D. A. (2003). *Labor Markets and Firm Benefit Policies in Japan and the United States (National Bureau of Economic Research Conference Report)* New York: University of Chicago Press.

Ogura, K. (2007). エンドレス・ワーカーズ : 働きすぎ日本人の実像. Tokyo: Nihon Keizai Shinbun Shuppansha.

Ohtsu, M. and Imanari, T. (2015). *Inside Japanese Business: A Narrative History, 1960-2000*. New York: Routledge. Omniglot (2019). *Japanese Hiragana*. https://www.omniglot.com/writing/japanese_hiragana.htm. Accessed July 29, 2019).

Onishi, N. (2005). *In Japan Crash, Time Obsession May Be Culprit*. The New York Times. 28 Apr. 2005. https://www.nytimes.com/2005/04/27/world/asia/in-japan-crash-time-obsession-may-be-culprit.html. Last accessed August 1, 2019.

Ono, H. (2010). *Lifetime Employment in Japan: Concepts and Measurement*. Journal of the Japanese and International Economies, Volume 24, No. 1, pp. 1-27.

Oohira, Y. (1998). *The Decision Pattern of the Enterprise of our Country: Yokonarabi (Homoegeneity)*. Bulletin of Shinshu Junior College, Volume 10, Issue 1-2, pp. 91-98.

Peltokorpi, V. (2006). *The Impact of Relational Diversity and Sociocultural Context on Interpersonal Communication: Nordic Subsidiaries in Japan*. Asian Business & Management, September 2006, Volume 5, Issue 3, pp. 333–356.

Persson, M. (2009). *Dealing with Sexual Harassment in the Workplace*. Japan Today. http://www.japantoday.com/category/commentary/view/dealing-with-sexual-harassment-in-the-workplace. Last accessed Dececember 11, 2009.

Pichler, R. (2008). The Three M's - The Lean Triad. http://www.infoq.com/articles/lean-muda-muri-mura. Last accessed August 19, 2019.

Pieper, R. (1990). *Human Resource Management: An International Comparison*. Berlin: Walter de Gruyter & Co.

Pye, M., Franke, E., Wasim, A. T. and M. Abdurrahman (2006). *Religious Harmony: Problems, Practice and Education*. Walter De Gruyter.

Rial, P. (2008) *Japan Cross-Shareholdings Send Investor Losses to $ 3.2 Billion*. Bloomberg, http://www.bloomberg.com/apps/news?pid=20601101&sid=akgw6DPNA0H4&refer=japan. Last accessed December 9, 2009).

Rebick, M. (2005). *The Japanese Employment System*. New York: Oxford University Press.

Rees, P. (2002). *Japan: The Missing Million*. BBC News. October 20, 2002. http://news.bbc.co.uk/2/hi/programmes/correspondent/2334893.stm. Accessed August 1, 2019.

Roger, J. D. and O. Ikeno (Eds.) (2002). *The Japanese Mind: Understanding Contemporary Japanese Culture*. Boston: Tuttle Publishing.

Rohlen, T. P. (1979). *For Harmony and Strength Japanese White-Collar Organization in Anthropological Perspective (Center for Japanese Studies)*. New York: University of California Press.

Saito, T. (2009). *Drawing out hikikomori: government youth outreach program a noble but narrow path*. The Mainichi Daily News, April 2009.

Sako, M. and Sato, H. (1997). *Japanese Labour and Management in Transition: Diversity, flexibility and participation*. New York: Routledge.

Sako, M. (2006). *Shifting Boundaries of the Firm Japanese Company - Japanese Labour*. Oxford: Oxford University Press.

Samovar, L. (2008). *Intercultural Communication: A Reader*. Wadsworth Publishing.

Schdot, Frederik. (1994). *America and the Four Japans, 1994, Friend, Foe, Model*. Berkeley: Mirror Stone Bridge Press.

Scher, M. (1999). *Bank-firm cross-shareholding in Japan: What is it, why does it matter, is it winding down?* DESA Discussion Paper No. 15. https://www.un.org/esa/desa/papers/2001/esa01dp15.pdf. Last accessed August 1, 2019.

Scheer, C. and P. Loos (2002). *Concepts of customer orientation - Internet business model for customer-driven output*. Proceedings of the 10th European Conference on Information Systems, Information Systems and the Future of the Digital Economy, ECIS 2002, Gdansk, Poland, June 6-8, 2002.

Shinohara, C. and Uggen, C. (2008). *Sexual Harassment: the emergence of legal consciousness in Japan and the U.S*. The Asia-Pacific Journal, Volume 31-2-09, August 3, 2008.

Scholtes, P. (1997). *The Leader's Handbook: Making Things Happen, Getting Things Done*. McGraw-Hill Education.

Schonberger, R. J. (1982). J*apanese Manufacturing Techniques*, New York: The Free Press.

Schonberger, R. J. (1983). *Applications of Single-Card and Dual-Card Kanban*. Interfaces 13.4, p. 56 - 67.

Seven&i Holdings. (2019). *Organization - Seven & I Holdings Co., Ltd*. Seven & i Holdings Co., Ltd. http://www.7andi.com/en/company/organization.html. Last accessed August 11, 2019.

shakaijin manâ kôza (2019). *shoukai suru toki no manâ*. http://manual.ranking5.com/hosoku/shoukai.html. Accessed August 1, 2019.

Sharpe, M. E. (2007). *The Old Japanese Keiretsu Model*. Japanese Economy, No. 34,3, p. 5-36.

Shinohara, C. and Uggen, C. (2008). *Sexual Harassment: the emergence of legal consciousness in Japan and the U.S*. The Asia-Pacific Journal, Volume 31-2-09, August 3, 2008.

Shiraiwa, H. (2018). *Japan aims to increase number of foreign-law attorneys*. Nikkei Asian Review, April 20, 2018. https://asia.nikkei.com/Politics/Japan-aims-to-increase-number-of-foreign-law-attorneys. Last accessed September 11, 2019.

Shook R. (1989). *Honda: An American Success Story*, Prentice Hall Direct.

Staff, J. (2009). *Kawaii Bento Boxes: Cute and Convenient Japanese Meals on the Go*. Japan Publications Trading.

Sugimori, Y., K. Kusunoki, F. Cho, and S. Uchikawa. (1977). *Toyota Production System and Kanban System Materialization of Just-In-Time and Respect-For-Human System*. International Journal of Production Research, No. 15,6 (1977): p. 553 - 64.

Sugiyama, S. (2019). *Government Bill on Power Harassment takes Aim at Japan's Workplace Woes*. Japan Times, March 28, 2019.

Sumi, S., Taniai, H., Miyachi, T. & Tanemura, M. (2006). *Sibling risk of pervasive developmental disorder estimated by means of an epidemiologic survey in Nagoya, Japan*. Journal of Human Genetics, June 2006, Volume 51, Issue 6, pp 518–522.

Sumitomo Corporation (2019). *Sumitomo History*. https://www.sumitomocorp.com/en/jp/about/company/sc-history/history. Last accessed August 1, 2019.

Tachibanaki, T. (1996). *Wage Determination and Distribution in Japan (1996)*. Oxford: Oxford University Press.

Tachibanaki, T. (2000). *Who Runs Japanese Business? Management and Motivation in the Firm*. Journal of Japanese Studies, January 2000, Volume 26, Issue 1, pp. 290-294.

Tanaka, Y. (2014). *The Family in Human Resource Management*. https://www.jil.go.jp/english/JLR/documents/2014/JLR44_tanaka.pdf. Last accessed August 1, 2019.

Taplin, R. (1995). *Decision-Making and Japan: A Study of Corporate Japanese Decision-Making and its Relevance to Western Companies*. London: Routledge.

The Economist (2009). *Genchi genbutsu*. Economist.com. http://www.economist.com/businessfinance/management/displaystory.cfm?story_id=14299017 (accessed August 11, 2019).

Tilin, A. (2005). *The Smartest Company of the Year*. CNNMoney.com http://money.cnn.com/magazines/business2/business2_archive/2005/01/01/8250213/index.htm. Last accessed December 17, 2009.

Totsuka, E. and T. Ueyanagi (2019). *Prevention of Death from Overwork and Remedies for Its Victims*. http://old.karoshi.jp/english/overwork1.html. Last accessed August 1, 2019.

Toyota (2019). *Toyota Production System. Company Vision & Philosophy Just-in-Time*. https://global.toyota/en/company/vision-and-philosophy/production-system/. Last accessed August 1, 2019.

Tsuji, S. (2008) *Designing of Effective English Training Programs in Japanese Corporations by the Use of Linguistic Auditing*. Jiyugaoka Sanno College Bulletin, No.41, 2008, p. 55 – 67.

Udayan, R. and Mourdoukoutas, P. (1994). *Job Rotation and Public Policy: Theory with Applications to Japan and the USA*. International Journal of Manpower, Volume 15, No. 6, pp. 57 - 71.

van Rixtel Adrian (2002). *Informality and Monetary Policy in Japan: The Political Economy of Bank Performance*. Cambridge: Cambridge University Press.

Varley, H. P. (2000). *Japanese Culture* (4th ed.). Honolulu: University of Hawaii Press.

Vogel, S. K (2006). *Japan Remodeled: How Government and Industry are Reforming Japanese Capitalism*. New York: Cornwell University Press. p78-114.'

Wikipedia (2009). *Vocational School*. http://en.wikipedia.org/wiki/Vocational_school. Last accessed August 1, 2019.

Wikipedia (2019a). *Education in the Empire of Japan*. http://en.wikipedia.org/wiki/Education_in_the_Empire_of_Japan. Last accessed August 23, 2019.
Wikipedia (2019b). 総合職 (*sôgôshoku*). http://ja.wikipedia.org/wiki/総合職. Last accessed August 1, 2019.
Wiltshire, R. (1995). *Relocating the Japanese worker: Geographical Perspectives on Personnel Transfers, Career Mobility and Economic Restructuring*. New York: Routledge.
Wisegeek (2019). *What is Karaoke?* http://www.wisegeek.com/what-is-karaoke.htm. Last accessed August 1, 2019.
Yamada, M. (1998). *Japan's Top Management from the Inside*. Palgrave Macmillan.
Yoshimura, N. and P. Anderson (1997). *Inside the Kaisha: Demystifying Japanese Business Behavior*. Boston: Harvard Business School Press.
Yoshiro, M. (1994). *Subcontracting Relationship (Shitauke Relationship) The Case of the Automobile Industry*. Working Paper. The University of Tokyo. http://www.cirje.e.u-tokyo.ac.jp/research/dp/94/f16/dp.pdf. Last accessed August 1, 2019.

Further Reading on Japanese Management

www.ingramcontent.com/pod-product-compliance
Lightning Source LLC
Chambersburg PA
CBHW071349210526
45465CB00001B/33